ARTIFICE, RUSE, AND SUBTERFUGE

THE EXPERT AT THE CARD TABLE
THE GRAPHIC ADAPTATION

A Treatise on the Science and Art of Manipulating Cards

BY

S.W. ERDNASE

Embracing the whole Calendar of Sleights that are Employed by the Gambler and Conjurer, describing with detail and illustration every known expedient, manoeuvre and stratagem of the Expert Card Handler, with over one hundred drawings from life by
M. D. Smith,
inked by
D.L. Trustman

PENCILS / INKS / LAYOUT
DAVID TRUSTMAN

ADAPTED & EDITED
BY
DAVID TRUSTMAN

PROOFREAD
BY
BRUCE BISHOP

2020

I'd like to dedicate this work to the hardest rock in the world, my son, Cooper, and to the my ever creative daughter, MJ.

NOTE
All of the text remains true to the original in content and structure. This IS The Expert at the Card Table.

EXTRA NOTE
Anything in these pages that is in a black balloon or box (other than figure numbers) is text not from the original and is meant as clarification.

COPYRIGHT

Artifice, Ruse, and Subterfuge, the Expert at the Card Table, the Graphic Novel, Copyright 2020, by David Trustman. All rights reserved.

ISBN-13   978-0-9978927-8-9

EXTRA-EXTRA NOTE
While all of the text does remain true to the original in content and structure, along with the new black clarification balloons, the story at the beginning and end wasn't from the original, and probably didn't happen to the real S.W. Erdnase. Except the Ninjas. That's definitely real.

INTRODUCTION. BY DAVID TRUSTMAN

I've always wanted to read THE EXPERT AT THE CARD TABLE. I've tried. Tried several times. Got the Dover edition. Got the amazing Darwin Ortiz annotated edition. From Darwin's edition, I still didn't learn any of Erdnase's sleights, but I learned that I should. Also, I learned Erdnase was interesting. Intriguing even. Next I got my hands on a copy of Revelation. I really wish I could say I read through it and learned something. I didn't. The EXPERT's content is dense, and not really written for someone like me. Finally, however, a couple weeks before Christmas of 2019, I figured out just how Erdnase could be read.

As midnight rolled around after a night of working on another book on memory, the realization struck me that I needed a break. The problem with a break though is what to do while breaking. How do you keep busy while doing nothing?

To fully understand the motivations that pushed me to opening Erdnase's book that night, I have to admit something personal. I'm a jealous person. Not in a bad way, mind you. I have a "challenge accepted" mindset where I see something I think is cool, and become jealous as to wishing I was the one capable of doing it. It was jealousy of the members of my Sunday card group (Kevin Reylek, Dennis Leung, Michael Bloemeke, and Will Jung, all of whom make me jealous in different ways,) that finally pushed me to delve into Erdnase.

I picked up Erdnase that late night, thinking that finally this was time I'd learn some carding! (a term of endearment for anything card related.) Like I said previously, I failed. Within twenty minutes I was scrolling through pictures of Chicago in 1900, trying to get an idea of what Erdnase would have been seeing if he was there way back when. A picture came across my screen of a nameless guy sitting in a chair, and it hit me. This was Erdnase. All someone had to do was draw him. All these years and no one had ever simply created a face for the author. S.W. Erdnase was a character and we would treat him as such. Erdnase's game of anonymity was to let the content of the book be the important aspect. We have agreed to play along!

The realization of just how to create a graphic edition of EXPERT struck like lightning. I love magic lectures. This would be an experience just like that. A large stock of images would be created. The goal would be a "single-camera" experience. Every paragragh would be broken down by sentence, and matched with talking or demonstration shots. Then, the coup de grace, the original figure drawings would be placed inside the new artwork. All I had to do was figure out how.

The figure drawings from EXPERT always irked me just a bit. The common style of art in magic books is to leave out the lines on the back of the hands. Some say this is "for clarity." Others say it is to follow the example set by M.D. Smith, the illustrator named for EXPERT. To me, however, I'm not a fan of simple hand illustrations. Whenever someone takes the time to add the tendons on the back of the hand, I'm far abler to grasp the angles required to accomplish the sleights.

Knowing my own preferences, I set out to modernize these original drawings. As a comic book artist, the different jobs related to creating art for publication are quite familiar to me. Drawing with pencils comes first, then inks which make the drawing ready for printing. With this in mind, the idea of updating the original figure drawings by creating new linework on top of the old, otherwise known as Pencilling and Inking, sprung to mind. This edition of EXPERT was just a slightly more complicated comic book!

After spending hours scanning the figures in, I discovered that someone else had already done it, and uploaded them for free on the internet. Each figure was enlarged, and converted to blue lines so that after they were pencilled and inked, they could be scanned without any unwanted linework. Groups of figure drawings were placed on pages of 11 x 17 card stock. Then the work started; re-pencilling, inking, scanning, clean-up, labelling, and finally placing them into the pages and illustrations.

This journey has changed me. I was once a frustrated, unsuccessful, wanna-be student of Erdnase. I am now a happy lover of his work. I understand what he was trying to teach and I am getting better every day. You can too.

Below you will find a list of things I discovered while taking the plunge into Erdnase.

> Almost all the cards used are Bridge sized cards. Only at the very end are Poker sized cards used.
> The hand model had small hands.
> The author talks about their small hands.
> Some of the figure drawings depict slim fingers while others have chunky fingers.
> The hands could belong to a short, middle-aged or heavier-set woman.
> None of the hands are of someone accustomed to manual labor.
> If an artist took the pencils home at night to ink them, the artist would only have themselves for a reference. Almost invariably hand drawings end up looking more like the artist's than the subject if the subject is separated from the artist.
> Two artists may have worked on the illustrations, or there were possibly long gaps in the production of the figure drawings. There is a significant difference in the underlying linework that you notice while looking at the figures, but really notice when you ink them.
> The bottom deal is hard and at the time of this writing I've only gotten it to work a few times when I can hit the right level of grip/relaxed grip that it requires. But every other sleight can be done. (By the time I got to the Legerdemain section I was breaking down every move and creating what I call "Point B hands"; hand illustrations that fill in the gaps. The point of this adaptation was to teach, and I at least broke everything down into the images that I needed to learn.)
> Erdnase had a witty sense of humor.
> Erdnase was a performer or was intimate with the concept of performing.
> Erdnase doesn't come off as a real stakes gambler, at least, not a gambler for stakes outside their circle of friends.
> The SWE Shift, the Longitudinal Shift, and the Erdnase One Handed Shift are amazingly fun to practice. The sleights in this book is genuinely fun to learn. Knacky, but fun. I was 39 at the start of this project, and I've learned the sleights. They take work. What doesn't that's worth it?
> The author was well read. Reading and practicing sleights with cards were featured prominently in their lives at least for a while.
> "Erdnase" could be two or more people. There is an instance where they state "the left hand" when meaning the right. With all their attention to detail, this seemed like an odd mistake. Half my monthly card group is left-handed. Half of Erdnase could've been too.
> I love "Erdnase." Because I have no idea the political or religious or worldview held by the actual author, I am free to blindly love this character known as Erdnase. The character flaws go only so far as what we know from the book. The sleights are incredible. The S.W.E. Shift is beyond incredible. (Especially if you use a prearranged order, wink wink, nudge nudge.)

I put A LOT of time and effort into these pages. I hope you enjoy my version of THE EXPERT AT THE CARD TABLE.

Special Thanks

I'd like to thank a few people for their input and tolerance during my very intense creation period of this book.

Betty and Stan Trustman

Mike Bekerman

Steve Beam

Shawn Martinbrough

Michael Bloemeke, Will Jung, Kevin Reylek, and Dennis Leung

IF I KNEW THEN WHAT I KNOW NOW...

Erdnase says that the Diagonal Palm-Shift should be acquired early. The Erdnase Single-Handed Shift, I think, is important to learn early not for the quality of the move itself, but for the confidence building it provides. It feels impossible, but isn't. Learn the Longitudinal and S.W.E. Shifts right away because they are insanely fun to practice, and then go back to the beginning. After learning the moves, go back and revisit Revelation and Darwin Ortiz's editions for fine tuning.

PART FIRST
CARD TABLE ARTIFICE
Table of Contents

S.W. ERDNASE

PREFACE 01	**TOP AND BOTTOM DEALING WITH ONE HAND** 38
INTRODUCTION 02	**SECOND DEALING** 39
CARD TABLE ARTIFICE 05	**ORDINARY METHODS OF STOCKING, LOCATING AND SECURING** 41
Professional Secrets 05	**STOCK SHUFFLE** 44
Hold Outs 07	**ERDNASE SYSTEM OF STOCK SHUFFLING** 46
Prepared Cards 07	Two-Card Stock 46
Confederacy 10	Three-Card Stock 48
Two Methods of Shuffling 11	Four-Card Stock 48
Primary Accomplishments 12	Five-Card Stock 50
Possibilities of the "Blind." 12	Twelve-Card Stock 50
Uniformity of Action 13	Euchre Stock 52
Deportment 13	**THE ERDNASE SYSTEM OF CULL SHUFFLING** 54
Display of Ability 13	To Cull Two Cards, Numbers 8, 4 55
Greatest Single Accomplishment 14	To Cull Three Cards, Numbers 7, 5, 9 55
Effect of Suspicion 14	To Cull Four Cards, Numbers 3, 6, 2, 5 56
Acquiring the Art 14	To Cull Nine Cards, Numbers 5, 1, 1, 1, 3, 1, 1, 7, 1 56
Importance of Details 15	**THE ERDNASE SYSTEM OF PALMING** 59
TECHNICAL TERMS 15	TOP PALM. First Method 59
ERDNASE SYSTEM OF BLIND SHUFFLES 18	TOP PALM. Second Method 60
POSITION FOR SHUFFLE 18	BOTTOM PALM. First Method 61
BLIND SHUFFLES 18	BOTTOM PALM. Second Method 62
I. To Retain Top Stock 19	BOTTOM PALM When Cards Are Riffled 63
II. To Retain Top Stock and Shuffle Whole Deck ... 21	Second Method 63
III. To Retain the Bottom Stock and Shuffle Whole Deck ... 21	**TO MAINTAIN THE BOTTOM PALM WHILE DEALING** ... 64
ERDNASE SYSTEM OF BLIND RIFFLES AND CUTS ... 22	**TO HOLD THE LOCATION OF CUT WHILE DEALING** ... 65
BLIND RIFFLES 23	**SHIFTS** 66
I. To Retain the Top Stock 23	**TWO-HANDED SHIFT** 67
II. To Retain the Bottom Stock 25	**THE ERDNASE SHIFT. One Hand** 68
BLIND CUTS 27	**ERDNASE SHIFT. Two Hands** 69
I. To Retain Bottom Stock. Top Losing One Card ... 27	**TO ASCERTAIN THE TOP CARDS WHILE RIFFLING AND RESERVE**
II. To Retain the Complete Stock 28	**THEM AT BOTTOM** 69
III. To Retain the Top Stock 29	**MODE OF HOLDING THE HAND** 70
IV. To Retain the Bottom Stock 30	**SKINNING THE HAND** 71
COMBINATION RIFFLE AND CUTS 31	**THE PLAYER WITHOUT AN ALLY** 73
V. To Retain Bottom Stock. Riffle II and Cut IV ... 31	Dealing Without the Cut 73
FANCY BLIND CUTS 31	Replacing the Cut as Before 73
I. To Retain the Complete Stock 31	Holding Out for the Cut 74
II. To Retain the Complete Stock 32	Shifting the Cut 74
ONE-HANDED FANCY TRUE CUT 32	Dealing Too Many 75
I. This is located by the Crimp 33	Crimping for the Cut 75
II. This is located by the jog 34	Replacing Palm When Cutting 76
III. This is located by the crimp 35	The Short Deck 77
IV. This is located by the jog 35	**THREE CARD MONTE** 78
BOTTOM DEALING 35	Mexican Three Card Monte 81

PART SECOND
LEGERDEMAIN
Table of Contents

LEGERDEMAIN	83
SHIFTS	85
Single-Handed Shift	85
The Longitudinal Shift	86
The Open Shift	87
The S.W.E. Shift	88
The Diagonal Palm Shift	89
THE BLIND SHUFFLE FOR SECURING SELECTED CARD	90
FORCING	91
PALMING	92
The Back Palm	92
CHANGES	93
The Top Change	93
The Bottom Change	93
The Palm Change	94
The Double-Palm Change	94
TRANSFORMATIONS. TWO HANDS	95
First Method	95
Second Method	95
Third Method	95
Fourth Method	96
Fifth Method	96
Sixth Method	96
TRANSFORMATIONS. ONE HAND	97
First Method	97
Second Method	98
BLIND SHUFFLES RETAINING ENTIRE ORDER	98
First Method	99
Second Method	100
Third Method	101
Fourth Method	101
Fifth Method	102
METHOD FOR DETERMINING A CARD THOUGHT OF	102
A. By the Riffle	102
B. By Springing Flourish	102
C. By the Cut	103
D. By the Gaze	103
TO GET SIGHT OF A SELECTED CARD	103
THE SLIDE	103
FAVORITE SLEIGHT FOR TERMINATING TRICKS	104
Catching Two Cards at Fingertips	104
Leaving Selected Card in Hand of Spectator	104
The Revolution	104
Cards Rising from the Hand	104
CARD TRICKS	105
Explanatory	105
The Exclusive Coterie	105
The Diving Rod	107
The Invisible Flight	108
TRICKS WITH A PREARRANGED DECK	109
The Traveling Cards	113
The Row of Ten Cards	115
The Acrobatic Jacks	116
A Mind-Reading Trick	117
Power of Concentrated Thought	118
The Acme of Control	119
The Card and Hankerchief	119
The Top and Bottom Production	119
The Three Aces	121
The Card and Hat	122

PREFACE

IN OFFERING THIS BOOK TO THE PUBLIC THE WRITER USES NO SOPHISTRY AS AN EXCUSE FOR ITS EXISTENCE.

THE HYPOCRITICAL CANT OF REFORMED (?) GAMBLERS, OR WHINING, MEALY-MOUTHED PRETENSIONS OF PIETY, ARE NOT FOISTED AS A JUSTIFICATION FOR IMPARTING THE KNOWLEDGE IT CONTAINS.

TO ALL LOVERS OF CARD GAMES IT SHOULD PROVE INTERESTING, AND AS A BASIS OF CARD ENTERTAINMENT IT IS PRACTICALLY INEXHAUSTIBLE.

IT MAY CAUTION THE UNWARY WHO ARE INNOCENT OF GUILE, AND IT MAY INSPIRE THE CRAFTY BY ENLIGHTENMENT ON ARTIFICE.

IT MAY DEMONSTRATE TO THE TYRO THAT HE CANNOT BEAT A MAN AT HIS OWN GAME, AND IT MAY ENABLE THE SKILLED IN DECEPTION TO TAKE A POST-GRADUATE COURSE IN THE HIGHEST AND MOST ARTISTIC BRANCHES OF HIS VOCATION.

BUT IT WILL NOT MAKE THE INNOCENT VICIOUS, OR TRANSFORM THE PASTIME PLAYER INTO A PROFESSIONAL; OR MAKE THE FOOL WISE, OR CURTAIL THE ANNUAL CROP OF SUCKERS; BUT WHATEVER THE RESULT MAY BE, IF IT SELLS IT WILL ACCOMPLISH THE PRIMARY MOTIVE OF THE AUTHOR, AS HE NEEDS THE MONEY.

INTRODUCTION

THE PASSION FOR PLAY IS PROBABLY AS OLD, AND WILL BE AS ENDURING, AS THE RACE OF MAN.

SOME OF US ARE TOO TIMID TO RISK A DOLLAR, BUT THE PERCENTAGE OF PEOPLE IN THIS FEVERISH NATION WHO WOULD NOT ENJOY WINNING ONE IS VERY SMALL.

THE PASSION CULMINATES IN THE PROFESSIONAL. HE WOULD RATHER PLAY THAN EAT. WINNING IS NOT HIS SOLE DELIGHT.

SOME ONE HAS REMARKED THAT THERE IS BUT ONE PLEASURE IN LIFE GREATER THAN WINNING, THAT IS, IN MAKING THE HAZARD.

TO BE SUCCESSFUL AT PLAY IS AS DIFFICULT AS TO SUCCEED IN ANY OTHER PURSUIT. THE LAWS OF CHANCE ARE AS IMMUTABLE AS THE LAWS OF NATURE.

WERE ALL GAMBLERS TO DEPEND ON LUCK THEY WOULD BREAK ABOUT EVEN IN THE END.

THE PROFESSIONAL CARD PLAYER MAY ENJOY THE AVERAGE LUCK, BUT IT IS DIFFICULT TO FIND ONE WHO THINKS HE DOES, AND IT IS INDEED WONDERFUL HOW MERE CHANCE WILL AT TIMES DEFEAT THE STRONGEST COMBINATION OF WIT AND SKILL.

IT IS ALMOST AN AXIOM THAT A NOVICE WILL WIN HIS FIRST STAKE.

A COLORED ATTENDANT OF A "CLUB-ROOM," OVERHEARING A DISCUSSION ABOUT RUNNING UP TWO HANDS AT POKER VENTURED THE FOLLOWING INTERPOLATION:

"DON'T TROUBLE BOUT NO TWO HAN'S, BOSS. GET YO' OWN HAN'. DE SUCKAH, HE'LL GET A HAN' ALL RIGHT, SUAH!"

AND MANY OLD PLAYERS BELIEVE THE SAME THING.

HOWEVER, THE VAGARIES OF LUCK, OR CHANCE, HAVE IMPRESSED THE PROFESSIONAL CARD PLAYER WITH A CERTAIN KNOWLEDGE THAT HIS MORE RESPECTED BROTHER OF THE STOCK EXCHANGE POSSESSES, VIZ.—

MANIPULATION IS MORE PROFITABLE THAN SPECULATION; SO TO MAKE BOTH ENDS MEET, AND INCIDENTALLY A GOOD LIVING, HE ALSO PERFORMS HIS PART WITH THE SHEARS WHEN THE LAMBS COME TO MARKET.

HAZARD AT PLAY CARRIES SENSATIONS THAT ONCE ENJOYED ARE RARELY FORGOTTEN.

THE WINNINGS ARE KNOWN AS "PRETTY MONEY," AND IT IS GENERALLY SPENT AS FREELY AS WATER.

THE AVERAGE PROFESSIONAL WHO IS SUCCESSFUL AT HIS OWN GAME WILL, WITH THE SUBLIMEST UNCONCERN, STAKE HIS MONEY ON THAT OF ANOTHER'S, THOUGH FULLY AWARE THE ODDS ARE AGAINST HIM.

HE KNOWS LITTLE OF THE REAL VALUE OF MONEY, AND AS A RULE IS GENEROUS, CARELESS AND IMPROVIDENT.

HE LOVES THE HAZARD RATHER THAN THE STAKES.

AS A MATTER OF FACT THE PRINCIPAL DIFFERENCE BETWEEN THE PROFESSIONAL GAMBLER AND THE OCCASIONAL GAMBLER, IS THAT THE FORMER IS ACTUATED BY HIS LOVE OF THE GAME AND THE LATTER BY CUPIDITY.

A PROFESSIONAL RARELY "SQUEALS" WHEN HE GETS THE WORST OF IT; THE MAN WHO HAS OTHER MEANS OF LIVELIHOOD IS THE HARDEST LOSER.

CARD TABLE ARTIFICE
PROFESSIONAL SECRETS.

ARTIFICE — CLEVER OR CUNNING DEVICES USED TO TRICK OR DECEIVE OTHERS.
— DICTIONARY DAVID

THE SECRETS OF PROFESSIONAL CARD PLAYING HAVE BEEN WELL PRESERVED.

WORKS ON CONJURING INVARIABLY DEVOTE MUCH SPACE TO THE CONSIDERATION OF CARD TRICKS, AND MANY HAVE BEEN WRITTEN EXCLUSIVELY FOR THAT PURPOSE, YET WE HAVE BEEN UNABLE TO FIND IN THE WHOLE CATEGORY MORE THAN AN INCIDENTAL REFERENCE TO ANY CARD TABLE ARTIFICE;

AND IN NO INSTANCE ARE THE PRINCIPAL FEATS EVEN MENTIONED.

SELF-STYLED "EX-PROFESSIONALS" HAVE REGALED THE PUBLIC WITH ASTOUNDING DISCLOSURES OF THEIR FORMER WILES AND WICKEDNESS, AND HAVE PROVEN A WONDERFUL KNOWLEDGE OF THE SUBJECT BY EXHUMING SOME ANTIQUATED MOSS-COVERED RUSES AS WELL KNOWN AS NURSERY RHYMES, AND EVEN THESE EXTRAORDINARY REVELATIONS ARE CALMLY DISMISSED WITH THE ASSERTION THAT THIS OR THAT ARTIFICE IS EMPLOYED; IN NOWISE ATTEMPTING TO EXPLAIN THE PROCESS OR GIVE THE DETAIL OF THE ACTION MENTIONED.

IF TERRIFIC DENUNCIATION OF ERSTWHILE ASSOCIATES, AND A DIATRIBE ON THE AWFUL CONSEQUENCES OF GAMBLING ARE A CRITERION OF ABILITY, THESE PURIFIED PRODIGALS MUST HAVE BEEN VERY DANGEROUS COMPANIONS AT THE CARD TABLE.

OF COURSE IT IS GENERALLY KNOWN THAT MUCH DECEPTION IS PRACTICED AT CARDS, BUT IT IS ONE THING TO HAVE THAT KNOWLEDGE AND QUITE ANOTHER TO OBTAIN A PERFECT UNDERSTANDING OF THE METHODS EMPLOYED, AND THE EXACT MANNER IN WHICH THEY ARE EXECUTED.

HENCE THIS WORK STANDS UNIQUE IN THE LIST OF CARD BOOKS. WE MODESTLY CLAIM ORIGINALITY FOR THE PARTICULAR MANNER OF ACCOMPLISHING MANY OF THE MANOEUVRES DESCRIBED, AND BELIEVE THEM VASTLY SUPERIOR TO OTHERS THAT HAVE COME UNDER OUR OBSERVATION.

WE DO NOT CLAIM TO KNOW IT ALL.

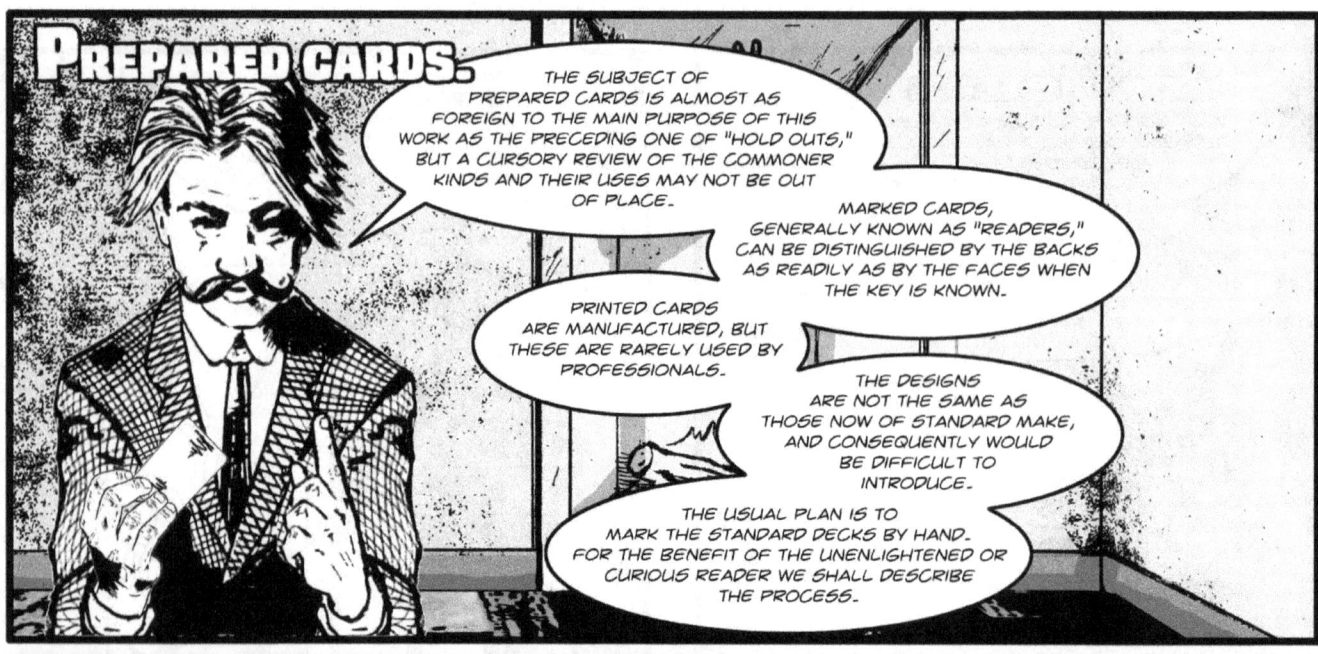

PREPARED CARDS.

THE SUBJECT OF PREPARED CARDS IS ALMOST AS FOREIGN TO THE MAIN PURPOSE OF THIS WORK AS THE PRECEDING ONE OF "HOLD OUTS," BUT A CURSORY REVIEW OF THE COMMONER KINDS AND THEIR USES MAY NOT BE OUT OF PLACE.

MARKED CARDS, GENERALLY KNOWN AS "READERS," CAN BE DISTINGUISHED BY THE BACKS AS READILY AS BY THE FACES WHEN THE KEY IS KNOWN.

PRINTED CARDS ARE MANUFACTURED, BUT THESE ARE RARELY USED BY PROFESSIONALS.

THE DESIGNS ARE NOT THE SAME AS THOSE NOW OF STANDARD MAKE, AND CONSEQUENTLY WOULD BE DIFFICULT TO INTRODUCE.

THE USUAL PLAN IS TO MARK THE STANDARD DECKS BY HAND. FOR THE BENEFIT OF THE UNENLIGHTENED OR CURIOUS READER WE SHALL DESCRIBE THE PROCESS.

IT IS NOT AT ALL DIFFICULT, AND A DECK CAN BE "DOCTORED" IN AN HOUR OR SO.

NEARLY ALL STANDARD CARDS ARE RED OR BLUE.

MARKING INKS ABSOLUTELY INDISTINGUISHABLE FROM THE PRINTER'S INK CAN BE OBTAINED FROM ANY OF THE DEALERS.

Jack of Spades. The left side is in an Erdnase-era style, while the right side is 1950's to current day. - Kevin "Card-Wiz" Reylek.

CARDS OF INTRICATE DESIGN ARE BEST ADAPTED FOR THE PURPOSE.

EACH CARD IS MARKED AT BOTH ENDS, SO AS TO BE READ IN ANY POSITION.

THE PECULIARITY OF THE FIGURES OR DESIGN ACROSS THE END IS FIRST CLOSELY CONSIDERED, AND TWELVE FAIRLY DISTINCT POINTS, OR DOTS OR DASHES, ARE NOTED AND LOCATED.

THEN THE FOUR ACES ARE LAID OUT, AND WITH A FINE PEN THE FIRST POINT LOCATED IS SHORTENED BARELY ENOUGH TO NOTICE.

THE POINT IS WHITE AND THE BACKGROUND RED OR BLUE, THE COLOR OF THE INK USED; AND THE SLIGHTEST SHORTENING OF A SINGLE POINT OR THE OBLITERATION OF A SINGLE DOT ON A CARD, IS UNDETECTABLE UNLESS IT IS KNOWN.

THE FOUR ACES ARE TREATED IN THIS MANNER, THEN TURNED END FOR END, AND THE OPERATION REPEATED.

THEN THE KINGS ARE DOCTORED, THE SECOND POINT LOCATED BEING SHORTENED IN THIS INSTANCE. THEN THE FOUR QUEENS AT THE THIRD POINT, AND SO ON THROUGHOUT THE DECK FOR THE TWELVE VALUES; THE ABSENCE OF ANY MARK DENOTING THE DEUCE.

NOW THE SUITS ARE MARKED. THREE ADDITIONAL POINTS ARE LOCATED, POSSIBLY CLOSE TO ONE CORNER. THE FIRST POINT MARKED SAY FOR DIAMONDS, THE SECOND FOR CLUBS, THIRD FOR HEARTS AND SPADES LEFT NATURAL.

THUS THE OPERATOR AT A GLANCE, BY NOTING THE LOCATION OF THE TWO "BLOCKOUTS," CAN INSTANTLY NAME THE CARDS AS THEY ARE DEALT.

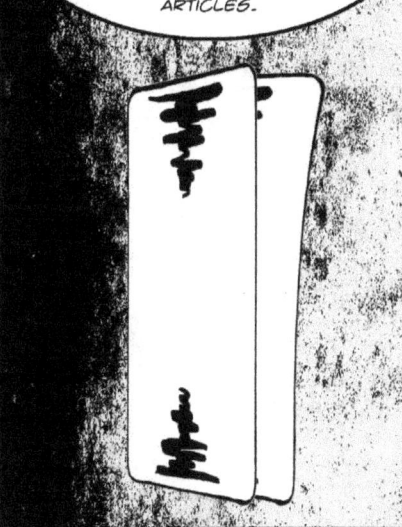

ADVANTAGES WITHOUT DEXTERITY CAN BE TAKEN IN ALMOST ANY CARD GAME WHEN TWO OR MORE PLAYERS ARE IN COLLUSION, BY THE USE OF ANY SECRET CODE OF SIGNALS THAT WILL DISCLOSE THE HAND OF EACH TO THE OTHERS.

FOR INSTANCE, IN POKER THE ALLY HOLDING THE BEST CARDS WILL BE THE ONLY ONE TO STAY, THUS PLAYING THE BEST HAND OF THE ALLIES AGAINST THE REST; QUITE SUFFICIENT ADVANTAGE TO GIVE A LARGE PERCENTAGE IN FAVOR OF THE COMBINATION.

AGAIN, THE ALLIES MAY RESORT TO "CROSSFIRING," BY EACH RAISING UNTIL THE OTHER PLAYERS DROP OUT.

THERE ARE HUNDREDS OF SMALL BUT ULTIMATELY CERTAIN ADVANTAGES TO BE GAINED IN THIS MANNER, IF COLLUSION IS NOT SUSPECTED.

NO SINGLE PLAYER CAN DEFEAT A COMBINATION, EVEN WHEN THE CARDS ARE NOT MANIPULATED.

TWO METHODS OF SHUFFLING.

AS THE READER OBTAINS AN UNDERSTANDING OF THE ART OF "ADVANTAGE PLAYING" IT WILL BE SEEN THAT THE OLD-FASHIONED OR HAND SHUFFLE GIVES THE GREATER POSSIBILITIES FOR RUNNING UP HANDS, SELECTING DESIRABLE CARDS AND PALMING.

MANY PLAYERS NEVER USE THE "RIFFLE," THAT IS SHUFFLING ON THE TABLE BY SPRINGING THE ENDS OF TWO PACKETS INTO EACH OTHER, THOUGH THIS METHOD IS NOW BY FAR THE MORE PREVALENT AMONG MEN WHO PLAY FOR MONEY.

WHILE THE "RIFFLE" CANNOT BE EMPLOYED FOR ARRANGING THE CARDS, SAVE TO A VERY LIMITED EXTENT, IT IS EQUALLY WELL ADAPTED FOR RETAINING THE TOP OR BOTTOM PORTION, OR EVEN THE WHOLE DECK, IN ANY PRE-ARRANGED ORDER; AND THE "BLIND RIFFLE" CAN BE PERFORMED JUST AS PERFECTLY AS THE "BLIND" SHUFFLE.

A CLEVER BOTTOM DEALER WILL USUALLY EMPLOY THE "RIFFLE," AS HE RARELY TAKES THE TROUBLE OF RUNNING UP A HAND.

HIS PURPOSE IN THAT RESPECT IS SUFFICIENTLY ANSWERED BY KEEPING THE DESIRED CARDS AT THE BOTTOM.

IF HE HAS AN ALLY TO "BLIND" CUT, EVERYTHING GOES WELL, BUT IF PLAYING ALONE HE MUST EITHER PALM THE BOTTOM CARDS FOR THE CUT OR MAKE A "SHIFT" AFTERWARDS.

THE "SHIFT" IS VERY RARELY ATTEMPTED IN ANY KIND OF KNOWING COMPANY, AND IT IS AWKWARD TO MAKE A PALM WHEN THE "RIFFLE" IS USED.

THE DECK MUST BE TILTED ON ITS SIDE, AND WHILE THE MOVEMENT MAY PASS AS AN EFFORT AT SQUARING UP, IT IS NOT QUITE REGULAR.

THE HAND SHUFFLE AVOIDS THE DIFFICULTY, AS THE DECK IS HELD NATURALLY IN EASY POSITION FOR PALMING, AND NOT AN INSTANT IS LOST DURING THE OPERATION.

THE HAND SHUFFLE IS ALMOST IDEAL FOR "STOCKING" AND "CULLING," AND THE CURIOUS OR INTERESTED READER MAY LEARN HOW A PERFECT KNOWLEDGE IS MAINTAINED OF THE WHEREABOUTS OF ANY PARTICULAR CARDS, AND HOW THEY ARE COLLECTED OR SEPARATED, OR PLACED IN ANY DESIRED POSITIONS, WHILE THE DECK IS BEING SHUFFLED APPARENTLY WITHOUT HEED OR DESIGN.

Primary Accomplishments.

The first acquirement of the professional player is proficiency at "blind" shuffling and cutting.

Perfection in performing the "blind" shuffle, whether the old-fashioned hand shuffle or the "riffle" supplemented by a thorough knowledge of "blind" cutting,

makes it impossible for the smartest card handler living to determine whether the procedure is true or "blind."

This ability once acquired gives the expert ease and assurance in any kind of company, and enables him to lull into a state of absolute serenity the minds of many players who may be naturally suspicious.

Nothing so completely satisfies the average card player as a belief that the deck has been thoroughly shuffled and genuinely cut.

Possibilities of the "Blind."

It is surprising to find among card players, and many of them grown gray at the game, the almost universal belief that none but the unsophisticated can be deceived by "blind" shuffling.

These gentlemen have to "be shown," but that is the last thing likely to happen.

The player who believes he cannot be deceived is in great danger.

The knowledge that no one is safe is his best protection.

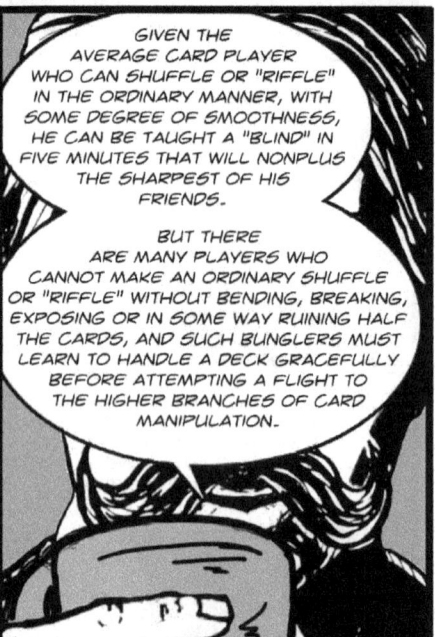

However, the post-graduate in the art is quite conscious of the fact that he himself cannot tell the true from the "blind" shuffle or cut, when performed by another equally as clever.

In fact, sight has absolutely nothing to do with the action, and the expert might perform the work just as well if he were blindfolded.

Nevertheless "blind" shuffling and cutting, as explained by this work, are among the simplest and easiest feats the professional player is required to perform; and when the process is understood the necessary skill can be acquired with very little time or effort.

Given the average card player who can shuffle or "riffle" in the ordinary manner, with some degree of smoothness, he can be taught a "blind" in five minutes that will nonplus the sharpest of his friends.

But there are many players who cannot make an ordinary shuffle or "riffle" without bending, breaking, exposing or in some way ruining half the cards, and such bunglers must learn to handle a deck gracefully before attempting a flight to the higher branches of card manipulation.

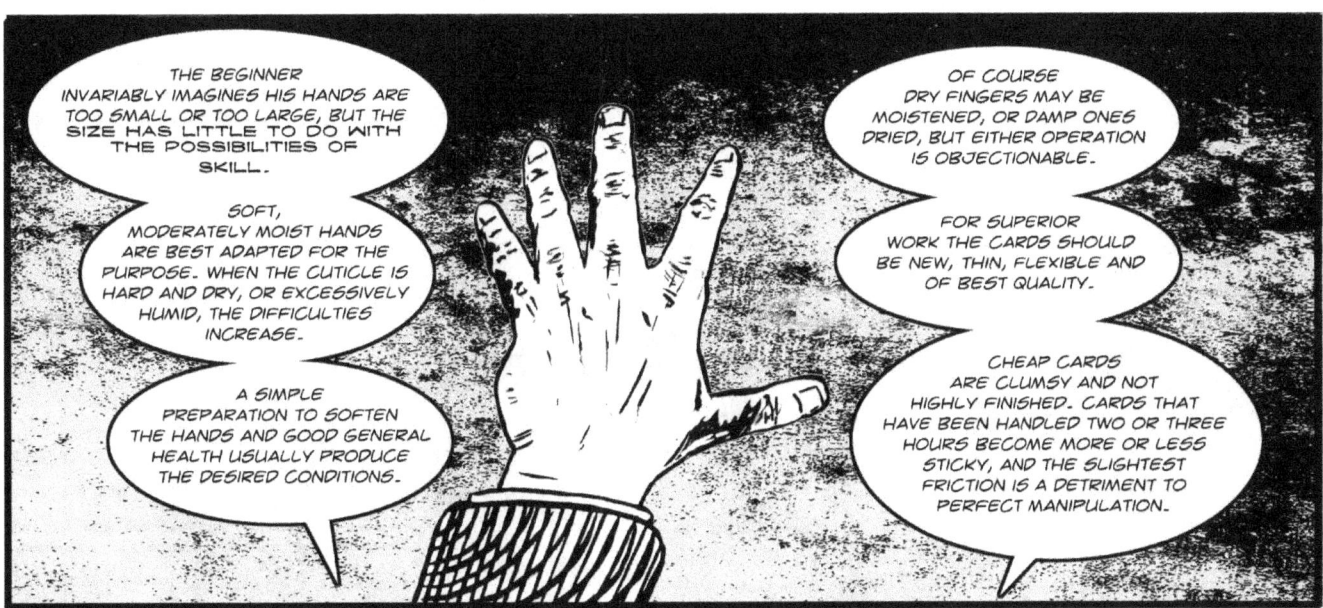

IMPORTANCE OF DETAILS.

TECHNICAL TERMS.

STOCK. THAT PORTION OF THE DECK THAT CONTAINS CERTAIN CARDS, PLACED IN SOME PARTICULAR ORDER FOR DEALING; OR CERTAIN DESIRABLE CARDS PLACED AT TOP OR BOTTOM OF THE DECK.

RUN. TO DRAW OFF ONE CARD AT A TIME DURING THE PROCESS OF THE HAND SHUFFLE.

THERE IS LITTLE OR NO DIFFICULTY IN ACQUIRING PERFECT ABILITY TO RUN THE WHOLE DECK THROUGH IN THIS MANNER WITH THE UTMOST RAPIDITY.

THE LEFT THUMB PRESSES LIGHTLY ON THE TOP CARD, THE RIGHT HAND ALONE MAKING THE MOVEMENT NECESSARY TO SHUFFLE.

JOG. A CARD PROTRUDING A LITTLE FROM ANY PART OF THE DECK, ABOUT QUARTER OF AN INCH, TO FIX THE LOCATION OF ANY PARTICULAR CARD OR CARDS.

WHILE SHUFFLING, IF THE TOP CARD IS TO BE JOGGED, IT IS PUSHED OVER THE LITTLE FINGER END OF DECK BY THE LEFT THUMB, THE LITTLE FINGER PREVENTING MORE THAN ONE CARD FROM MOVING.

IF THE FIRST CARD IS TO BE JOGGED, THAT IS, THE FIRST CARD IN THE RIGHT HAND, IT IS DONE BY SHIFTING THE RIGHT HAND SLIGHTLY TOWARDS EITHER END OF THE LEFT HAND PACKET DURING THE SHUFFLE, SO THAT THE FIRST CARD DRAWN OFF BY THE LEFT THUMB WILL PROTRUDE A LITTLE OVER THE END OF THE LEFT-HAND PACKET.

IN-JOG. THE CARD PROTRUDING OVER THE LITTLE FINGER OF THE LEFT HAND.

OUT-JOG. THE CARD PROTRUDING OVER THE FIRST FINGER OF THE LEFT HAND.

BREAK. A SPACE OR DIVISION HELD IN THE DECK. WHILE SHUFFLING IT IS HELD AT THE END BY THE RIGHT THUMB. IT IS FORMED UNDER THE IN-JOG WHEN ABOUT TO UNDER-CUT FOR THE SHUFFLE, BY PUSHING THE IN-JOG CARD SLIGHTLY UPWARDS WITH THE RIGHT THUMB, MAKING A SPACE OF FROM AN EIGHTH TO A QUARTER OF AN INCH WIDE, AND HOLDING THE SPACE, BY SQUEEZING THE ENDS OF THE PACKET TO BE DRAWN OUT, BETWEEN THE THUMB AND SECOND AND THIRD FINGERS.

THE USE OF THE BREAK DURING A SHUFFLE MAKES IT POSSIBLE TO THROW ANY NUMBER OF CARDS THAT ARE IMMEDIATELY ABOVE IT, IN ONE PACKET INTO THE LEFT HAND, WITHOUT DISARRANGING THEIR ORDER.

THE BREAK IS USED WHEN NOT SHUFFLING, TO LOCATE ANY PARTICULAR CARD OR POSITION, AND IS INFINITELY SUPERIOR TO THE COMMON METHOD OF INSERTING THE LITTLE FINGER.

A BREAK CAN BE HELD FIRMLY BY A FINGER OR THUMB OF EITHER HAND, AND ENTIRELY CONCEALED BY THE OTHER FINGERS OF THE SAME HAND.

IT IS ALSO THE PRINCIPAL AID IN THE BLIND RIFFLES AND CUTS.

THROW. TO PASS FROM THE RIGHT HAND TO THE LEFT, DURING A SHUFFLE, A CERTAIN NUMBER OF CARDS IN ONE PACKET, THEREBY RETAINING THEIR ORDER.

A THROW MAY BE REQUIRED AT THE BEGINNING, DURING THE PROCESS, OR AT THE END OF A SHUFFLE; AND THE PACKET TO BE THROWN MAY BE LOCATED BY THE JOG, OR BREAK, OR BY BOTH.

CULLS. THE DESIRED CARDS. TO CULL IS THE ACT OF SELECTING ONE OR MORE DESIRED CARDS, AND MAY CONSIST SIMPLY IN MAKING THE SELECTION AS DISCREETLY AS POSSIBLE WHILE GATHERING UP THE CARDS FOR THE DEAL, OR IT MAY BE THE OPERATION OF A MUCH MORE OBSCURE AND APPARENTLY IMPOSSIBLE FEAT—THAT OF GATHERING THE DESIRED CARDS RAPIDLY AND EASILY, FROM VARIOUS POSITIONS IN THE DECK, TO THE BOTTOM, DURING THE PROCESS OF A SHUFFLE THAT APPEARS PERFECTLY NATURAL AND REGULAR.

BLIND. ANY METHOD OF SHUFFLING, RIFFLING, CUTTING OR CULLING, DESIGNED TO APPEAR REGULAR, BUT IN REALITY RETAINING, OR ARRANGING, SOME PRECONCEIVED ORDER.

UPPER CUT. TO TAKE OR DRAW OFF A PACKET FROM THE TOP OF THE DECK.

UNDER CUT. TO DRAW OUT A PACKET FROM THE BOTTOM OF THE DECK, DURING THE PROCESS OF A SHUFFLE.

RUN CUT. TO DRAW OFF SEVERAL OR MANY SMALL PACKETS FROM THE TOP OF THE DECK.

TOP CARD.—THE CARD ON TOP OF PACKET HELD IN THE LEFT HAND, OR THE ORIGINAL TOP CARD OF THE FULL DECK, WHICH IS ABOUT TO BE SHUFFLED.

FIRST CARD. THE CARD ON TOP OF PACKET HELD BY THE RIGHT HAND TO BE SHUFFLED.

SHUFFLE. THE OLD-FASHIONED METHOD OF SHUFFLING THE CARDS FROM HAND TO HAND.

SHUFFLE OFF.—TO SHUFFLE WITHOUT DESIGN, IN THE ORDINARY MANNER.

RIFFLE.—THE MODERN METHOD OF SHUFFLING ON THE TABLE BY SPRINGING THE ENDS OF TWO PACKETS INTO EACH OTHER.

SHIFT.—TO RETURN THE TWO PORTIONS OF THE DECK TO THE POSITIONS OCCUPIED BEFORE THE CUT WAS MADE.

CRIMP.—TO BEND ONE OR A NUMBER OF CARDS, SO THAT THEY MAY BE DISTINGUISHED OR LOCATED.

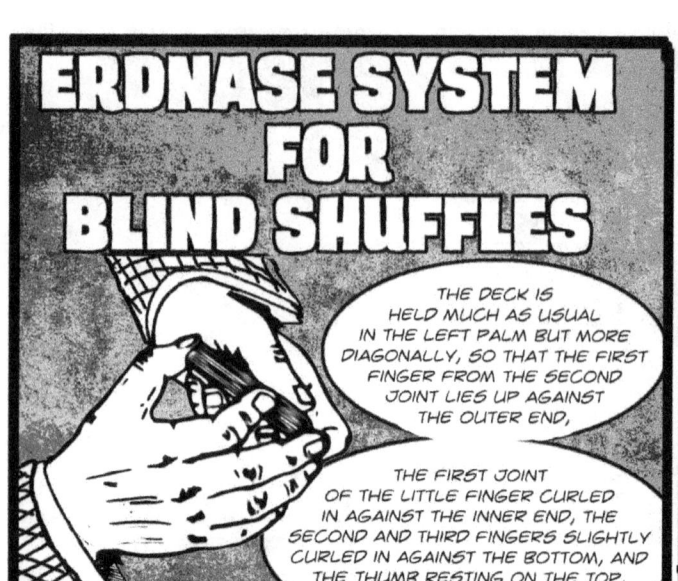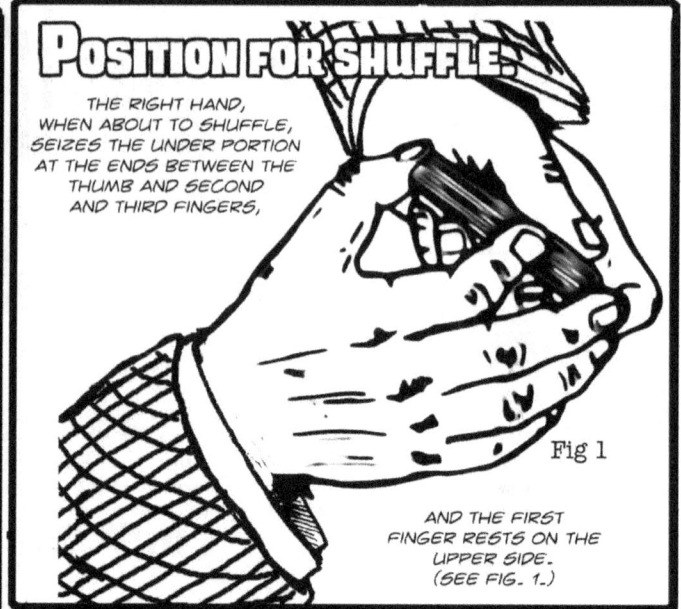

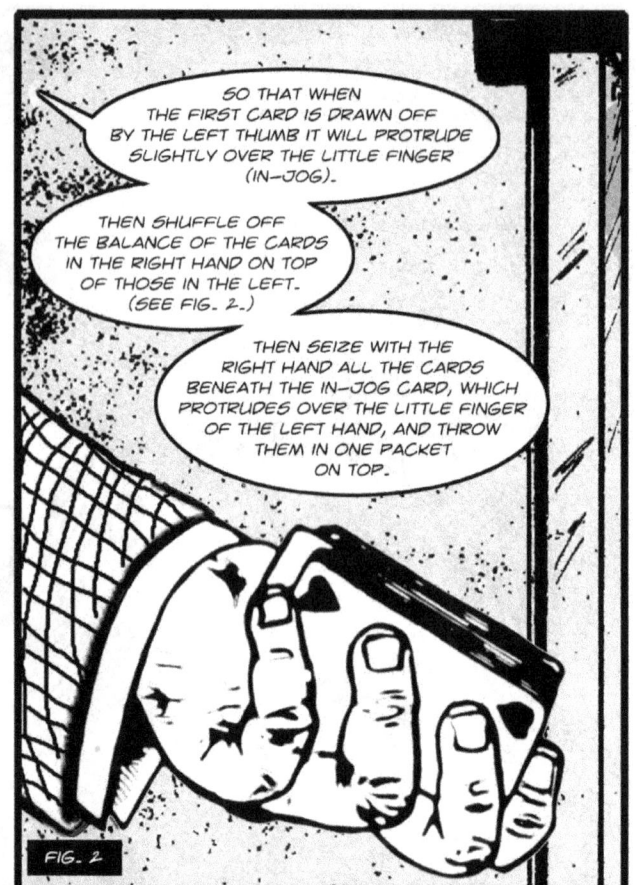

Fig. 3

II.- TO RETAIN TOP STOCK AND SHUFFLE WHOLE DECK

UNDER CUT ABOUT THREE-QUARTERS OF DECK, IN-JOG FIRST CARD AND SHUFFLE OFF.

Fig. 3

UNDER-CUT AGAIN ABOUT THREE-QUARTERS OF DECK, FORMING BREAK AT IN-JOG (SEE FIG. 3), SHUFFLE OFF TO BREAK AND THROW BALANCE ON TOP.

THIS BLIND APPARENTLY SHUFFLES THE ENTIRE DECK, BUT REALLY LEAVES THE TOP PORTION IN THE ORIGINAL ORDER.

THERE SHOULD BE NO DIFFICULTY IN FORMING THE BREAK. THE RIGHT THUMB PRESSES SLIGHTLY UPWARD ON THE IN-JOG CARD WHEN SEIZING THE UNDER PORTION, AND THE SPACE CREATED IS HELD BY SQUEEZING THE ENDS.

IT SHOULD BE DONE ALTOGETHER BY TOUCH, ALTHOUGH FROM THE POSITION IT IS IN, THE OPERATOR MIGHT GLANCE AT IT WITHOUT BEING NOTICED.

IT IS PRACTICALLY IMPOSSIBLE FOR A SPECTATOR TO SEE IT UNLESS IMMEDIATELY BEHIND THE PERFORMER.

WHEN SHUFFLING OFF TO THE BREAK, THE RIGHT HAND HOLDS THE CARDS FIRMLY AND THE RIGHT THUMB GIVES THE WARNING BY THE SENSE OF TOUCH WHEN THE BREAK IS REACHED.

IF DESIRED, THE RIGHT HAND MAY SHUFFLE OFF, QUITE CARELESSLY, SEVERAL CARDS AT A TIME, AND THROW THE LAST LOT UP TO THE BREAK, BY SLIGHTLY DECREASING THE PRESSURE ON THE ENDS. ABOVE ALL, A UNIFORMITY OF TIME AND ACTION MUST BE MAINTAINED, THOUGH IT IS NOT AT ALL ESSENTIAL TO THE BLIND TO SHUFFLE RAPIDLY.

III. TO RETAIN THE BOTTOM STOCK AND SHUFFLE WHOLE DECK.

UNDER-CUT ABOUT THREE-QUARTERS OF THE DECK AND SHUFFLE OFF ABOUT TWO-THIRDS, THEN IN-JOG ONE CARD AND THROW BALANCE ON TOP.

UNDER-CUT TO AND INCLUDE IN-JOG CARD (SEE FIG. 4), AND SHUFFLE OFF.

Fig. 4

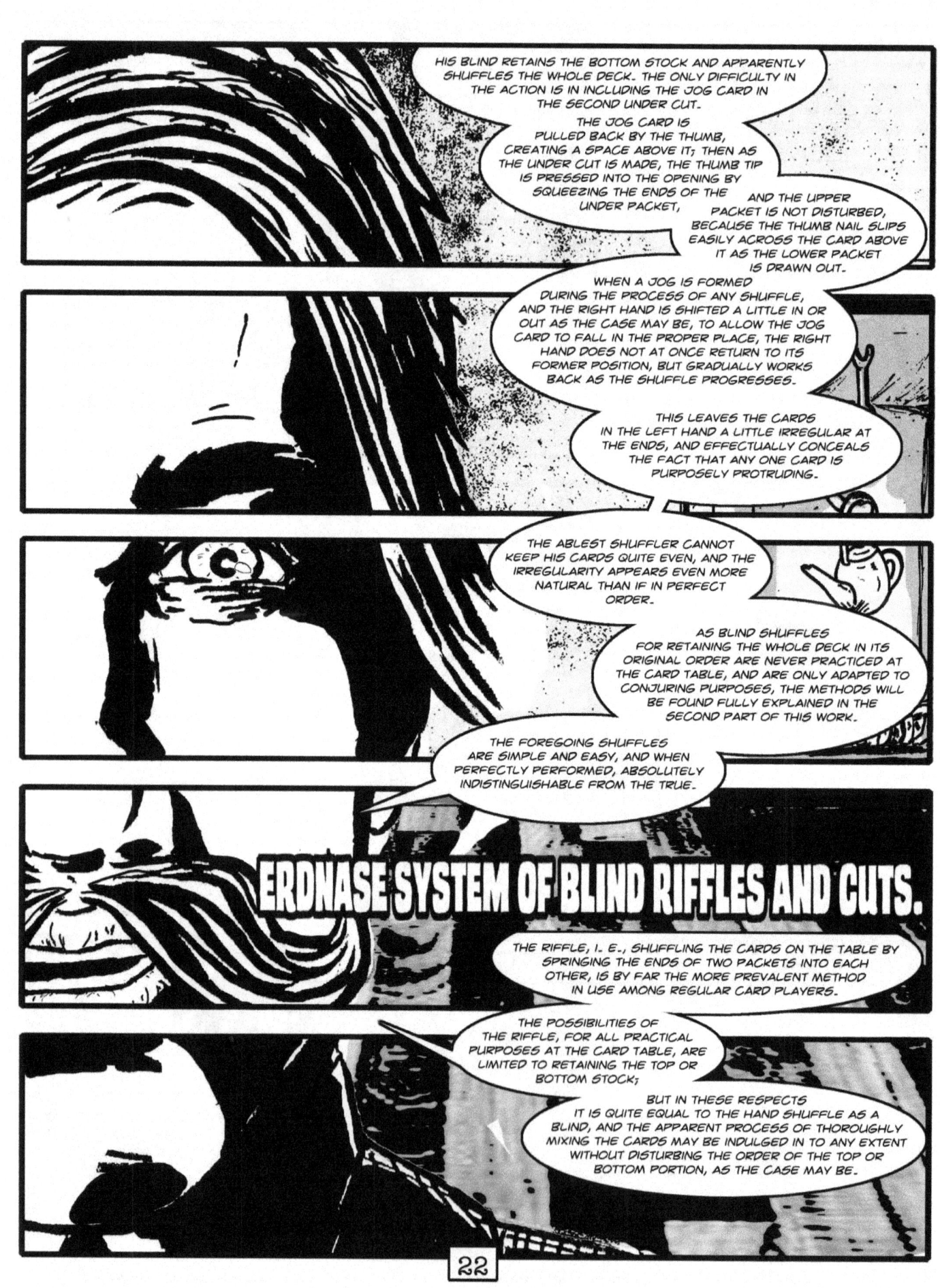

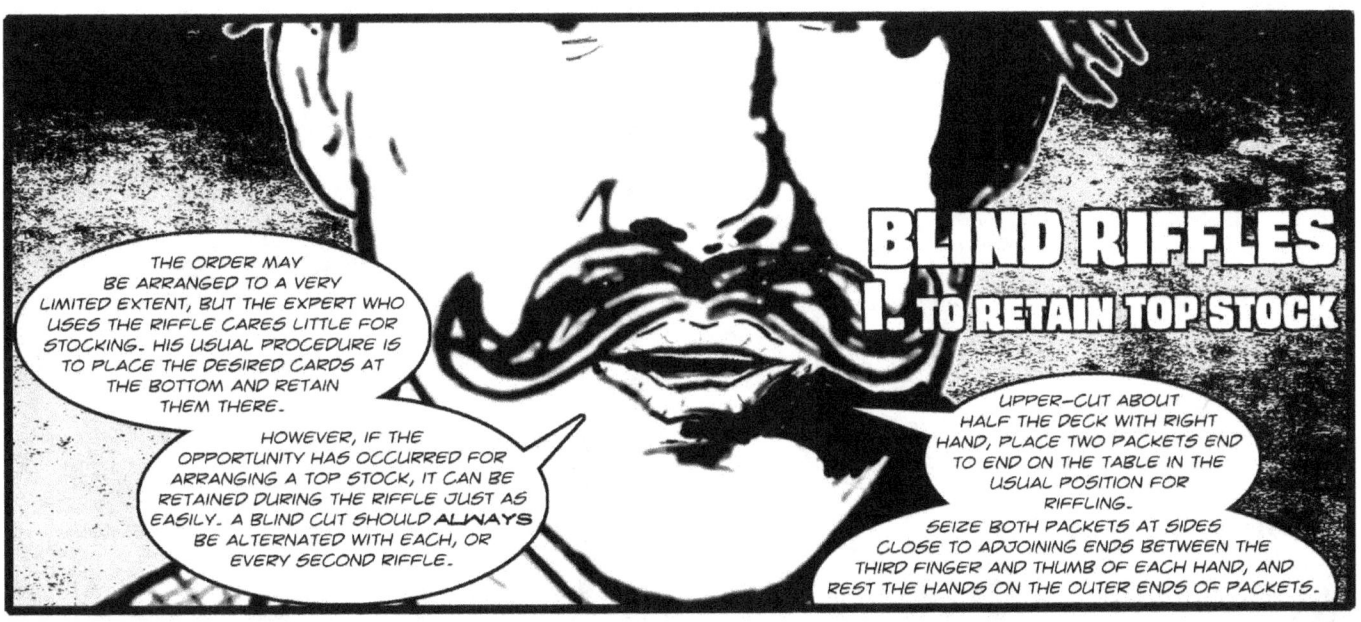

BLIND RIFFLES
1. TO RETAIN TOP STOCK

THE ORDER MAY BE ARRANGED TO A VERY LIMITED EXTENT, BUT THE EXPERT WHO USES THE RIFFLE CARES LITTLE FOR STOCKING. HIS USUAL PROCEDURE IS TO PLACE THE DESIRED CARDS AT THE BOTTOM AND RETAIN THEM THERE.

HOWEVER, IF THE OPPORTUNITY HAS OCCURRED FOR ARRANGING A TOP STOCK, IT CAN BE RETAINED DURING THE RIFFLE JUST AS EASILY. A BLIND CUT SHOULD **ALWAYS** BE ALTERNATED WITH EACH, OR EVERY SECOND RIFFLE.

UPPER-CUT ABOUT HALF THE DECK WITH RIGHT HAND, PLACE TWO PACKETS END TO END ON THE TABLE IN THE USUAL POSITION FOR RIFFLING.

SEIZE BOTH PACKETS AT SIDES CLOSE TO ADJOINING ENDS BETWEEN THE THIRD FINGER AND THUMB OF EACH HAND, AND REST THE HANDS ON THE OUTER ENDS OF PACKETS.

RAISE THE THUMB CORNERS, AND AT THE SAME MOMENT IN-JOG THE TOP CARD OF THE LEFT-HAND PACKET BY DRAWING IT IN A LITTLE OVER THE LEFT THUMB, WITH THE FIRST FINGER OF THE LEFT HAND.

THE FIRST AND SECOND FINGERS OF THE LEFT HAND CONCEAL BOTH THE JOG AND THE ACTION. (SEE FIG. 5.)

THEN BEGIN TO RELEASE, AND SPRING OR RIFFLE INTO EACH OTHER THE ENDS OF THE LOWER CARDS WITH BOTH THUMBS, BUT MORE RAPIDLY WITH THE LEFT THUMB, SO THAT THE LEFT PACKET,

WITH THE EXCEPTION OF THE TOP CARD (WHICH IS RETAINED ON TOP OF THE LEFT THUMB) WILL HAVE BEEN RIFFLED IN BEFORE THE RIGHT THUMB HAS RELEASED THE CARDS OF THE TOP STOCK.

Fig. 5

CONTINUE THE ACTION WITH THE RIGHT THUMB UNTIL ALL ARE RELEASED, THEN RELEASE LAST CARD HELD BY THE LEFT THUMB. (SEE FIG. 6.)

THIS ACTION PLACES ONE EXTRA CARD ON ORIGINAL TOP STOCK. TO SQUARE UP IN THE ORDINARY MANNER WOULD EXPOSE THE FACT THAT THE UPPER PORTION HAD NOT BEEN RIFFLED.

DROP THE LEFT THUMB ON THE TOP CARD TO HOLD THE DECK IN POSITION AND SHIFT THE LEFT HAND SO THAT THE EDGE OF THE PALM WILL REST ON THE TABLE AT THE END OF THE LEFT PACKET AND THE SECOND AND THIRD FINGERS COME ALONG THE SIDE.

Fig. 6

Fig. 7

"Then with the right hand in much the same position as the left, but held more openly, push the right packet in and square up. (See Fig. 7.)"

"Each time this riffle is made it leaves an extra card on top,"

"and the top stock is usually arranged to require two or three extra cards."

"But if not required the extra card is gotten rid of by 'Blind Cut No. I.' After each or every second riffle execute Blind Cut 'No. III to retain the top stock.'"

"This riffle, though requiring considerable explanation, is quite simple, and as easily executed as the true."

"There is no hesitation in the thumb action, although one moves more rapidly than the other."

"The movements are NATURAL; the positions of the hands are REGULAR, and even the manner of pushing in the cards is the customary one of many players."

"But, as intimated, to retain the top stock in the riffle is the exception."

"In most instances, when the blind is used, it is to retain the bottom stock, and that process which is next described, is even simpler and easier of execution, and more perfect in deception."

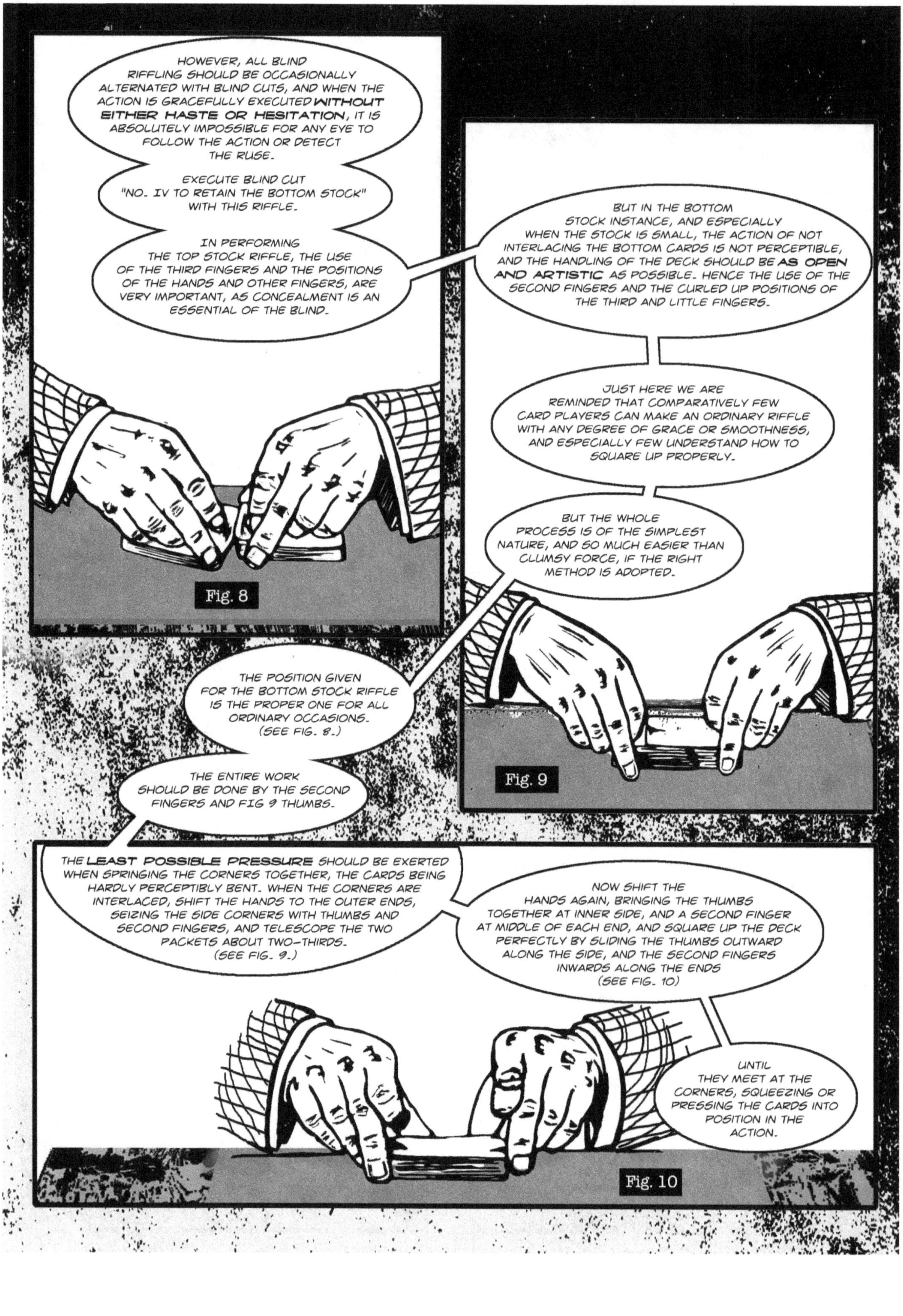

However, all blind riffling should be occasionally alternated with blind cuts, and when the action is gracefully executed **without either haste or hesitation**, it is absolutely impossible for any eye to follow the action or detect the ruse.

Execute blind cut "No. IV to retain the bottom stock" with this riffle.

In performing the top stock riffle, the use of the third fingers and the positions of the hands and other fingers, are very important, as concealment is an essential of the blind.

But in the bottom stock instance, and especially when the stock is small, the action of not interlacing the bottom cards is not perceptible, and the handling of the deck should be **as open and artistic** as possible. Hence the use of the second fingers and the curled up positions of the third and little fingers.

Just here we are reminded that comparatively few card players can make an ordinary riffle with any degree of grace or smoothness, and especially few understand how to square up properly.

But the whole process is of the simplest nature, and so much easier than clumsy force, if the right method is adopted.

Fig. 8

The position given for the bottom stock riffle is the proper one for all ordinary occasions. (See Fig. 8.)

The entire work should be done by the second fingers and Fig 9 thumbs.

Fig. 9

The **least possible pressure** should be exerted when springing the corners together, the cards being hardly perceptibly bent. When the corners are interlaced, shift the hands to the outer ends, seizing the side corners with thumbs and second fingers, and telescope the two packets about two-thirds. (See Fig. 9.)

Now shift the hands again, bringing the thumbs together at inner side, and a second finger at middle of each end, and square up the deck perfectly by sliding the thumbs outward along the side, and the second fingers inwards along the ends (See Fig. 10)

Until they meet at the corners, squeezing or pressing the cards into position in the action.

Fig. 10

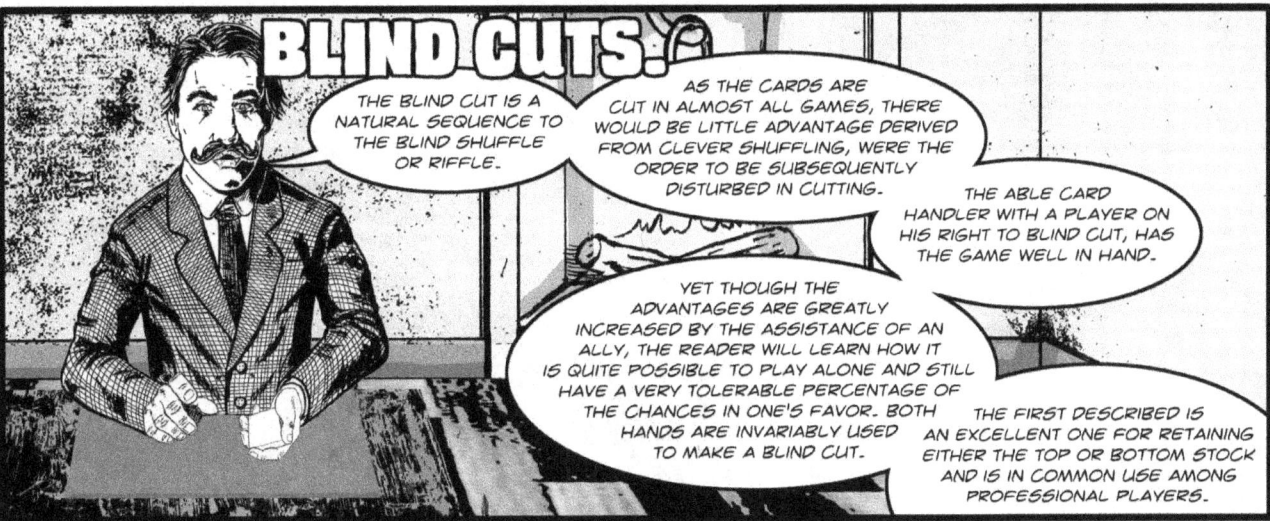

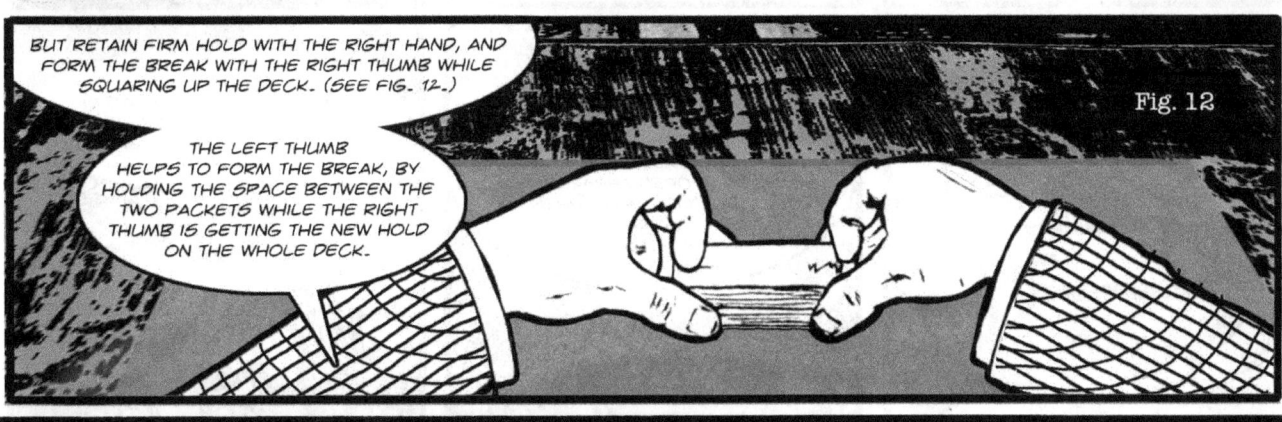

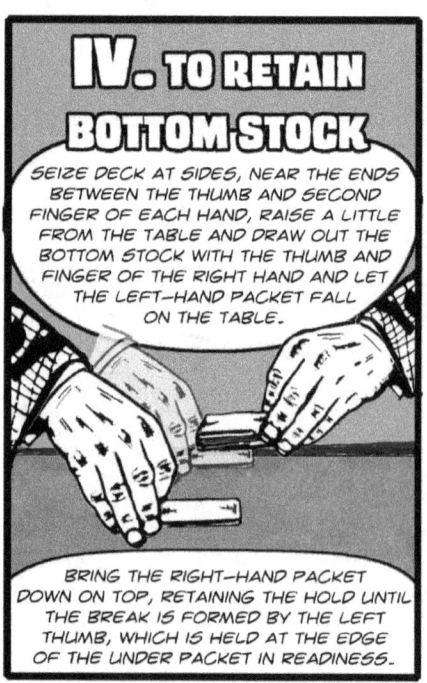

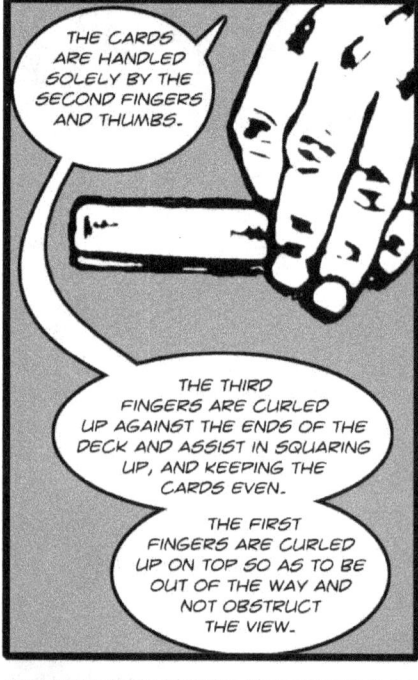
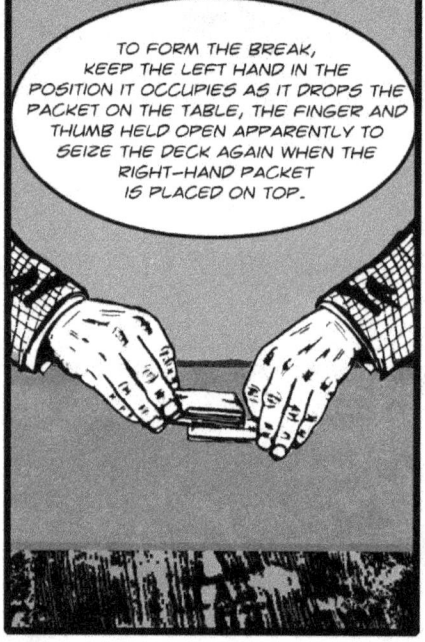

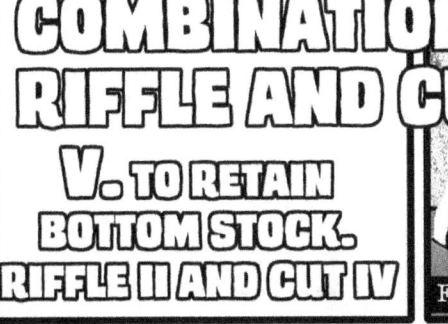

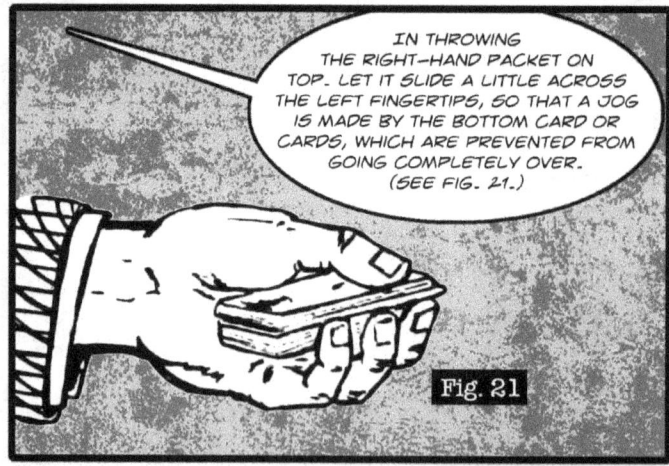

III. THIS LOCATED BY THE CRIMP.

WHEN THE RIFFLE IS USED, THE CRIMP IS PUT IN BY FIRST CONCAVING THE WHOLE DECK.

THIS IS A NATURAL PROCEDURE, AS THE CARDS HAVE A TENDENCY TO GET CONVEX, AND IT IS QUITE CUSTOMARY FOR THE PLAYERS TO STRAIGHTEN THEM UP.

BY DRAWING THE DECK TO THE EDGE OF THE TABLE THE CONCAVE TENDENCY CAN BE PUT IN THE WHOLE DECK FIRST, THEN AS THE EXTRA CUT IS MADE A CONVEX CRIMP CAN BE PUT IN THE UNDER PART BY PRESSING IT QUICKLY DOWNWARDS WITH RIGHT THUMB AGAINST THE TABLE EDGE AS IT IS DRAWN OUT.

THE ALLY CUTS BY THE ENDS.

IV. THIS IS LOCATED BY THE JOG.

PERHAPS THE BEST MANNER OF LOCATING THE CUT WHEN THE RIFFLE IS USED, IS TO JOG THE TOP CARD BY PUSHING IT SLIGHTLY OVER THE RIGHT-HAND END, WITH THE LEFT FIRST FINGER.

THEN MAKE THE EXTRA CUT WITH THE RIGHT HAND, THROWING THE UNDER PORTION ON TOP, AND SQUARING UP AT SIDES AND LEFT-HAND END ONLY.

THE DECK IS PASSED TO THE ALLY BY THE SIDES WITH THE RIGHT HAND, WHICH CONCEALS THE JOGGED CARD. THE ALLY CUTS BY THE ENDS, HIS THUMB EASILY LOCATING THE JOG, AND SEIZING THE PACKET ABOVE IT.

THE PARTICULAR MANNER IN WHICH THE DEALER FORMS THE CRIMP, OR JOG, TO LOCATE THE CUT, MATTERS LITTLE IF IT IS DONE IN A NATURAL MANNER AND WITHOUT ATTRACTING ATTENTION.

BUT A SINGLE IRREGULAR MOVEMENT, OR A MOMENT'S HESITATION, MAY RUIN THE PLAY.

HENCE, HOWEVER SIMPLE AND EASY THE PARTICULAR ACTION MAY BE, THE EXECUTION SHOULD BE CAREFULLY PLANNED AND PRACTICED BEFOREHAND, AND WHEN PUT INTO EFFECT SHOULD BE PERFORMED ALMOST MECHANICALLY.

FOR THESE REASONS WE HAVE DEVOTED MUCH SPACE TO MANY DETAILS THAT MAY AT FIRST APPEAR OF LITTLE MOMENT.

BOTTOM DEALING

THE ART OF DEALING FROM THE BOTTOM, ALTHOUGH NOT THE MOST DIFFICULT TO ATTAIN, IS PERHAPS THE MOST HIGHLY PRIZED ACCOMPLISHMENT IN THE REPERTORY OF THE PROFESSIONAL.

THE BOTTOM IS THE MOST CONVENIENT PLACE FOR RETAINING DESIRABLE CARDS DURING THE SHUFFLE OR RIFFLE, AND PERFECTION IN DEALING FROM THAT POSITION OBVIATES TO A GREAT EXTENT THE NECESSITY OF STOCKING, AS THE CARDS CAN BE DEALT AT WILL, AND CONSEQUENTLY NEED NOT BE RUN UP IN A CERTAIN ORDER.

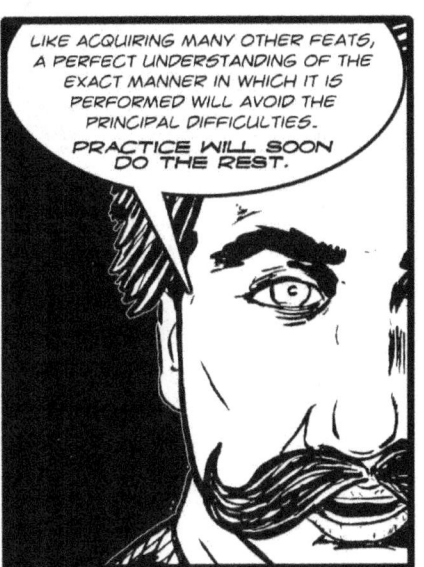

LIKE ACQUIRING MANY OTHER FEATS, A PERFECT UNDERSTANDING OF THE EXACT MANNER IN WHICH IT IS PERFORMED WILL AVOID THE PRINCIPAL DIFFICULTIES.

PRACTICE WILL SOON DO THE REST.

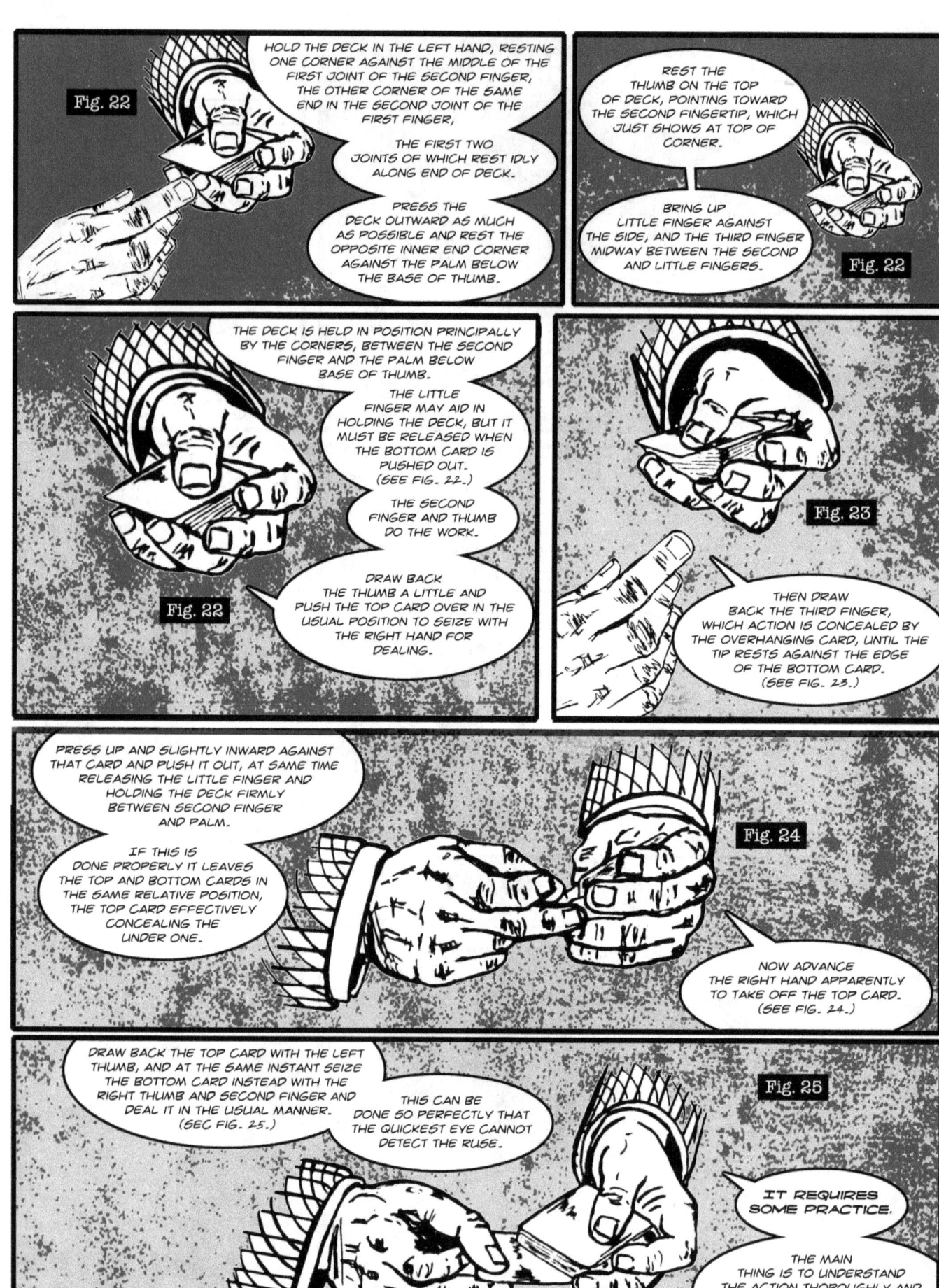

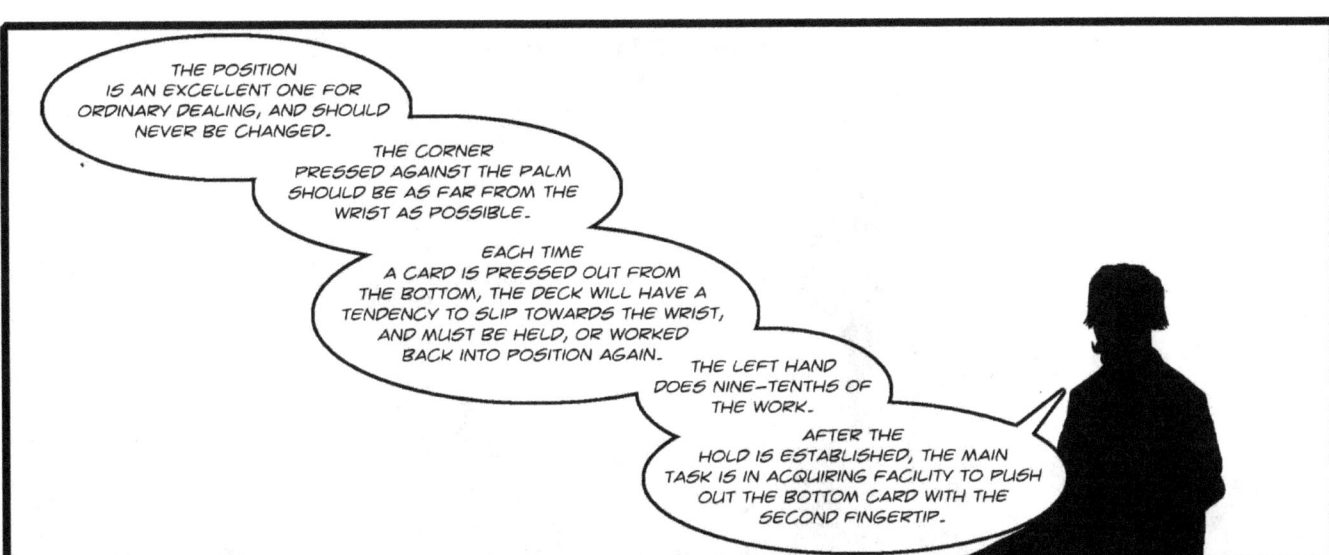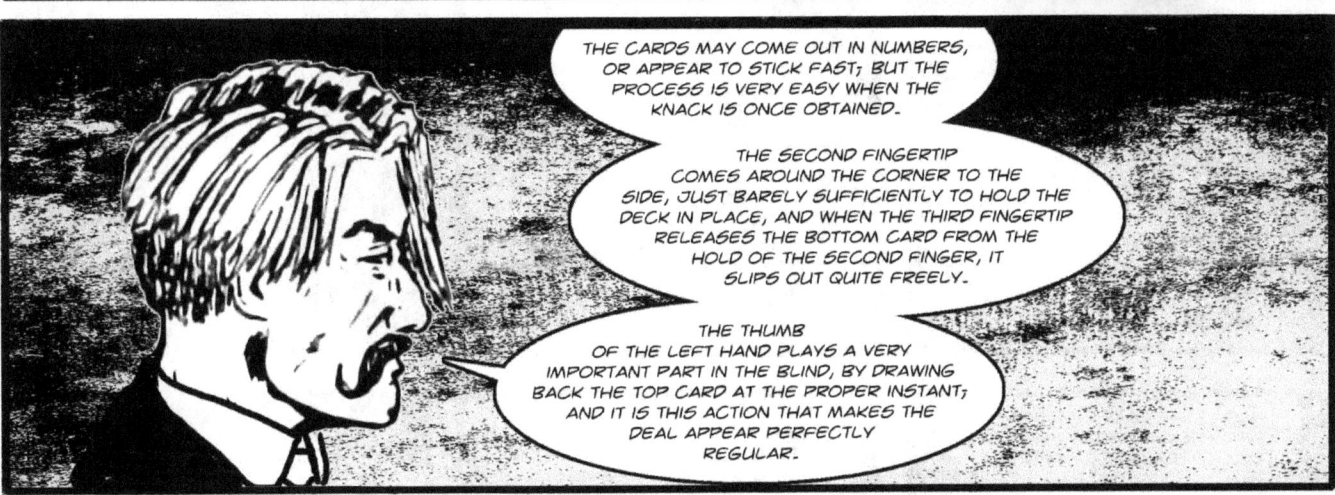

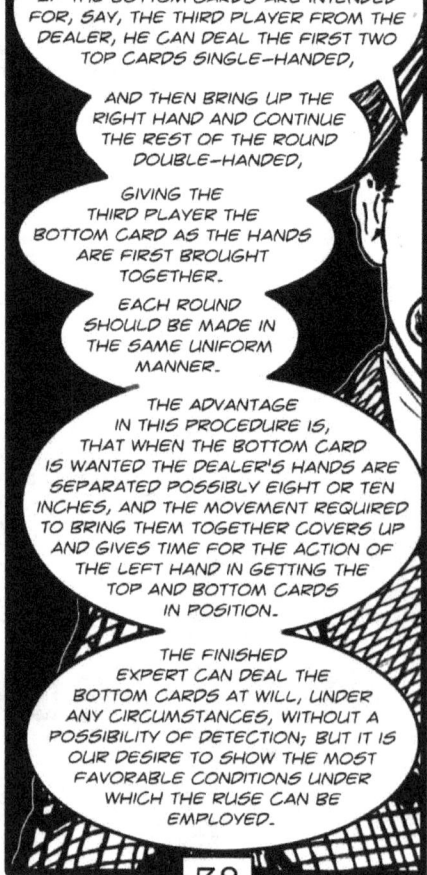

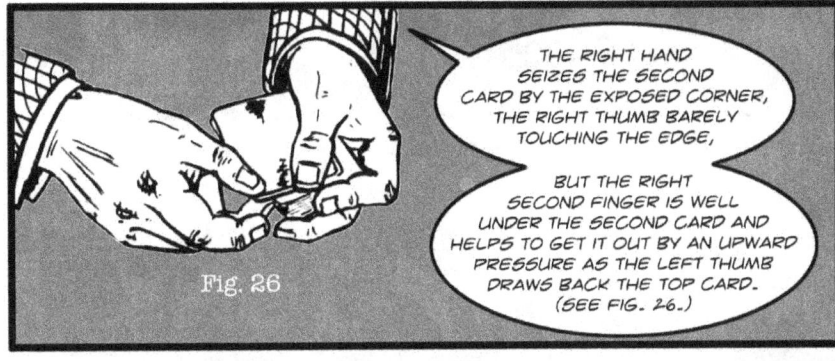
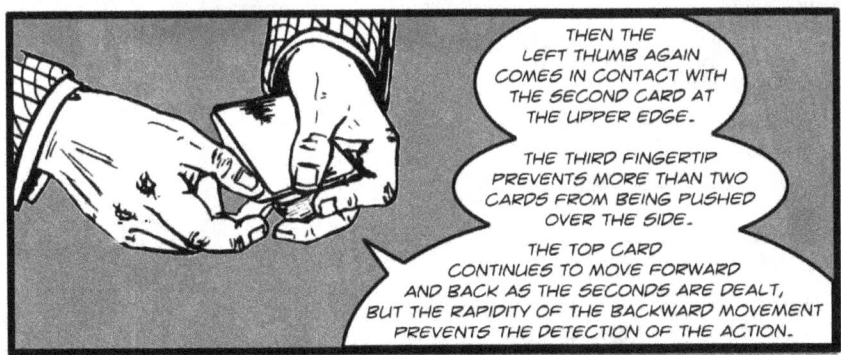

ANOTHER METHOD OF SECOND DEALING IS TO HOLD THE CARDS LOOSELY IN THE LEFT HAND, THE LEFT THUMB PUSHING FORWARD SEVERAL AT A TIME, EACH A LITTLE IN ADVANCE OF THE OTHER.

AS THE RIGHT HAND COMES FORWARD, THE TOP CARD IS DRAWN BACK AND THE SECOND DEALT.

THE LEFT THUMB USES SOME PRESSURE IN PUSHING THE CARDS FORWARD, BUT DRAWS BACK THE TOP CARD VERY LIGHTLY SO AS TO HAVE THE SECOND CARD PROTRUDING. (SEE FIG. 27.)

Fig. 27

THE FIRST METHOD IS DECIDEDLY THE BETTER, AS IT GIVES GREATER CONTROL OF THE CARDS, AND THERE IS LESS LIABILITY OF THE RIGHT HAND SEIZING MORE THAN ONE.

THERE IS A KNACK IN SEIZING THE SECOND CARD.

THE SECOND FINGER OF THE RIGHT HAND COMES IN CONTACT WITH IT BEFORE THE TOP CARD IS DRAWN BACK, AND GIVES IT A SLIGHT PRESSURE UPWARD, THUS HELPING TO PREVENT IT GOING BACK WITH THE TOP CARD.

THE RIGHT THUMB MAY ACTUALLY TOUCH THE TOP CARD AS IT IS DRAWN BACK AND THE SECOND DEALT.

THE WHOLE ACTION OF DRAWING BACK THE TOP AND DEALING THE SECOND CARD TAKES PLACE AT THE SAME INSTANT.

TO BECOME AN ADEPT AT SECOND DEALING IS AS DIFFICULT A TASK AS CAN BE GIVEN IN CARD HANDLING, BUT ONCE ACQUIRED, LIKE MANY OTHER ARTS, IT IS AS EASY AS HABIT.

TO THE PLAYER WHO USES MARKED CARDS THIS ACCOMPLISHMENT IS THE WHOLE THING, BUT WITHOUT "READERS" THE TIME SPENT IN ACQUIRING THE SKILL IS WASTED AS FAR AS ADVANTAGE PLAYING IS CONCERNED.

OPPORTUNITIES FOR INTRODUCING PREPARED CARDS ARE RARE, AND THE PROCESS OF MARKING DURING A GAME, BY CREASE, CRIMP, OR INKING, IS SLOW AND DETECTABLE.

HOWEVER, WITH "READERS," "STRIPPERS," OR ANY KIND OF PREPARED CARDS THE CLEVER PROFESSIONAL WHO VALUES HIS REPUTATION WILL HAVE NOTHING TO DO.

ORDINARY METHODS OF STOCKING, LOCATING AND SECURING

THE MOST ORDINARY MODE OF STOCKING CONSISTS IN ARRANGING THE CARDS AS DISCREETLY AS POSSIBLE WHILE TAKING TRICKS, OR MAKING THE DISCARD, OR WHILE GATHERING UP FOR THE DEAL.

THERE IS NO SLEIGHT OF HAND IN THIS.

A PLAYER, IF HE KEEPS HIS WITS ABOUT HIM, FINDS MANY OPPORTUNITIES DURING A SITTING OF PREARRANGING TO SOME EXTENT FOR HIS DEAL.

WITH THE AID OF A PARTNER OF COURSE THE POSSIBILITIES ARE DOUBLED.

BUT THE GENERAL UNDERSTANDING IS THAT THE WHOLE DECK MUST BE TAMPERED WITH BEFORE THE SHUFFLE BEGINS.

IF DALLIANCE WITH THE DECK IS ALLOWED, AND IT IS AMAZING HOW MUCH OF THAT SORT OF THING IS PERMITTED IN SOME GAMES, A PRACTICED OPERATOR CAN RUN UP ONE OR TWO HANDS WITH INCREDIBLE RAPIDITY, AND HIS ACTIONS WILL APPEAR AS MERE TRIFLING.

Fig. 28

THIS IS DONE BY HOLDING THE DECK IN THE LEFT HAND, BACK TO PALM, WITH THUMB AGAINST ONE SIDE, SECOND, THIRD AND LITTLE FINGERS ON THE OTHER SIDE, AND FIRST FINGER CURLED UP AGAINST THE BACK. THE RIGHT HAND NOW COVERS THE FACE, FINGERS AT ONE END, THUMB AT THE OTHER.

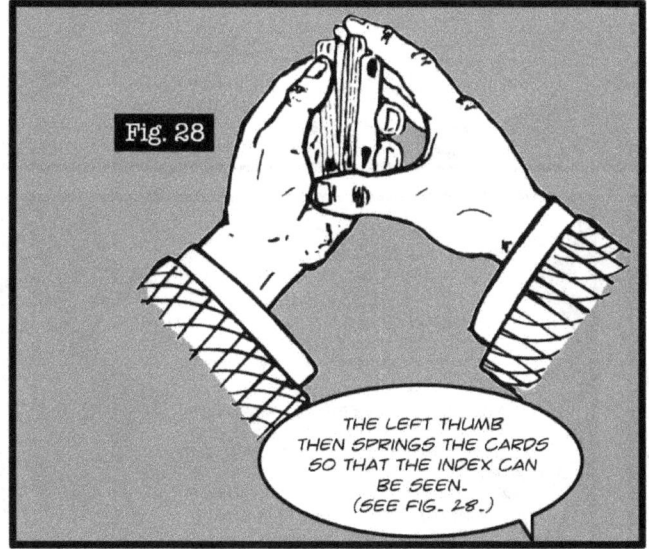

Fig. 28

THE LEFT THUMB THEN SPRINGS THE CARDS SO THAT THE INDEX CAN BE SEEN. (SEE FIG. 28.)

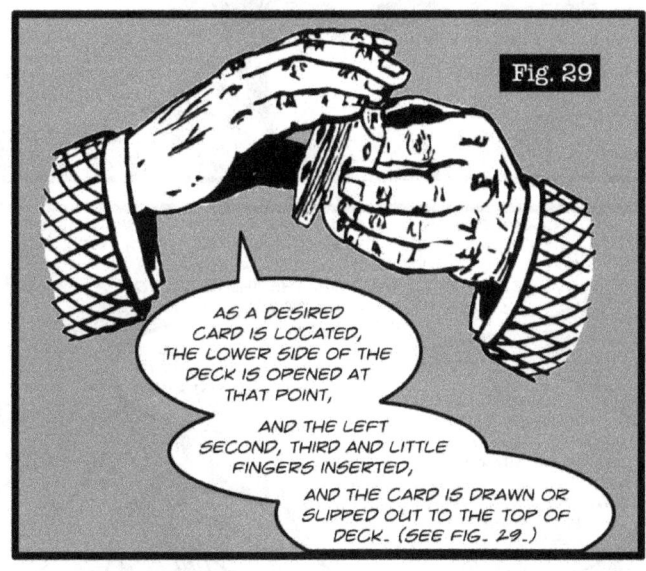

Fig. 29

AS A DESIRED CARD IS LOCATED, THE LOWER SIDE OF THE DECK IS OPENED AT THAT POINT, AND THE LEFT SECOND, THIRD AND LITTLE FINGERS INSERTED, AND THE CARD IS DRAWN OR SLIPPED OUT TO THE TOP OF DECK. (SEE FIG. 29.)

THEN INDIFFERENT CARDS TO THE REQUISITE NUMBER ARE SLIPPED FROM THE BOTTOM IN THE SAME MANNER ON TOP OF THE FIRST SELECTED CARD.

THEN THE NEXT DESIRED CARD IS LOCATED AND BROUGHT TO THE TOP, AND SO ON TILL THE STOCK IS COMPLETE.

LITTLE OR NO SKILL IS REQUIRED, BUT A PRACTICED HAND CAN LOCATE AND BRING THE CARDS TO THE TOP IN A MOMENT OR TWO AND WITHOUT THE LEAST NOISE.

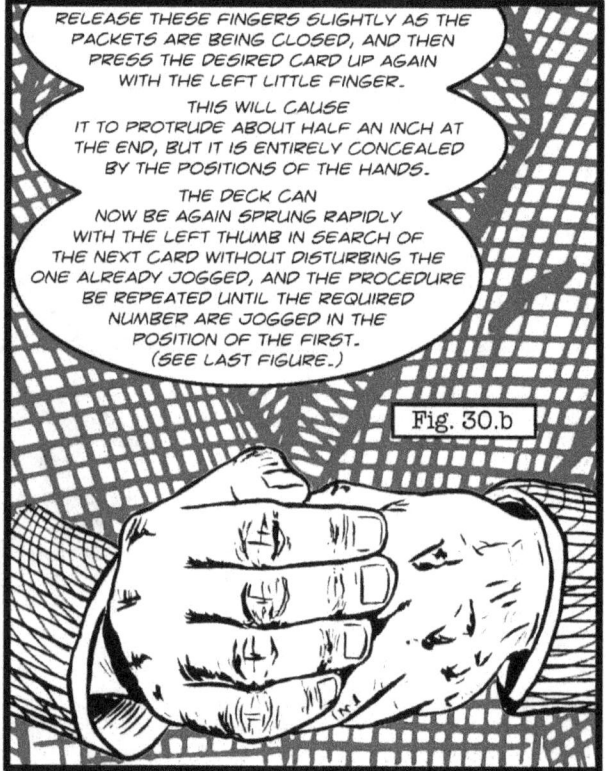

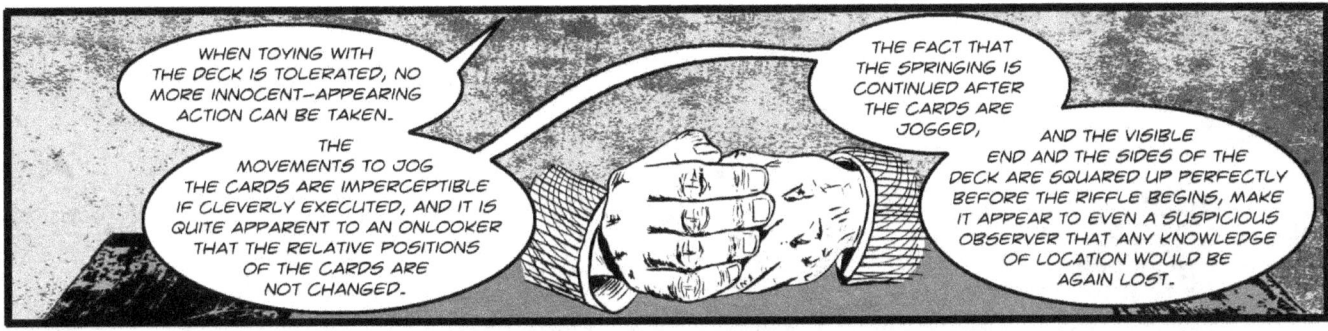

Fig. 30.c

Fig. 31

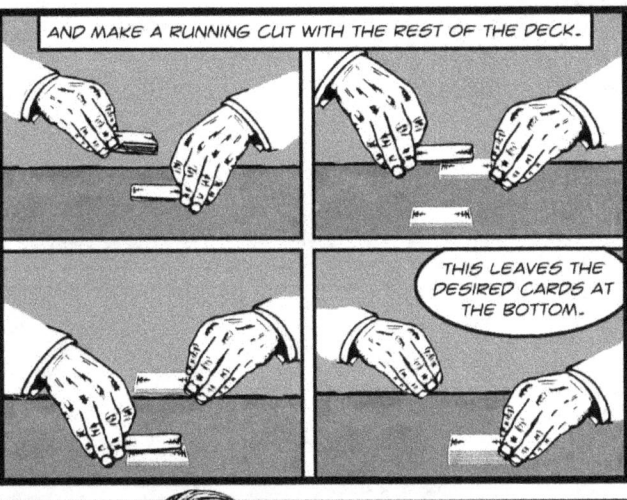

Fig. 31

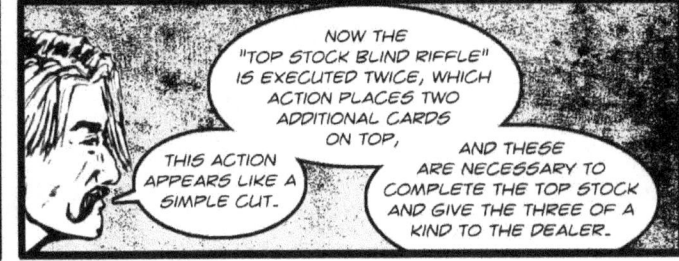

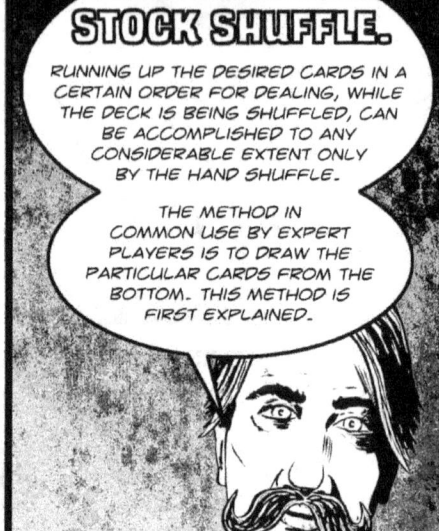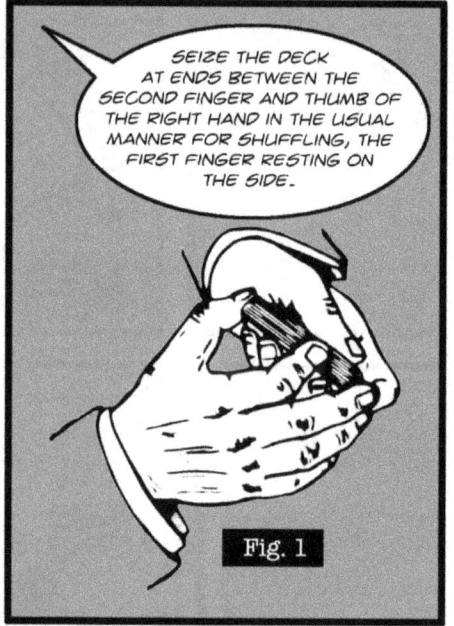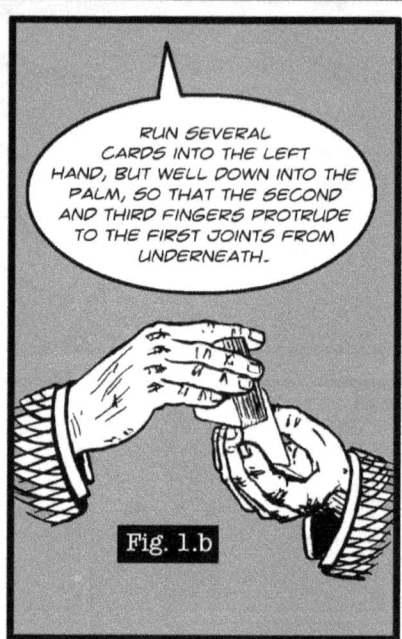

THIS EXAMPLE, OF COURSE, IS FOR A GAME IN WHICH THE CARDS ARE DEALT ONE AT A TIME TO EACH PLAYER.

IF THE GAME REQUIRES TWO OR MORE CARDS AT A TIME THE ACTION IS THE SAME BUT MERELY REPEATED.

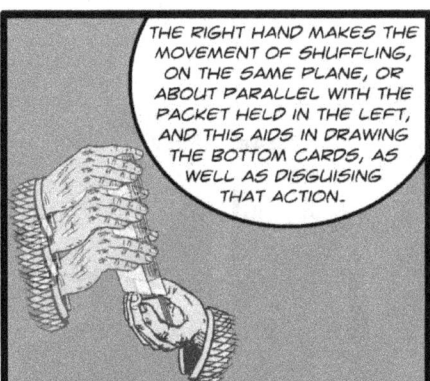

THE RIGHT HAND MAKES THE MOVEMENT OF SHUFFLING, ON THE SAME PLANE, OR ABOUT PARALLEL WITH THE PACKET HELD IN THE LEFT, AND THIS AIDS IN DRAWING THE BOTTOM CARDS, AS WELL AS DISGUISING THAT ACTION.

THERE IS A LITTLE DIFFERENCE IN THE SOUND AS THE CARDS FALL FROM THE TOP AND BOTTOM, BUT IT IS HARDLY NOTICEABLE.

THIS METHOD REQUIRES CONSIDERABLE PRACTICE, AS THE KNACK OF DRAWING THE BOTTOM CARDS, AND BUT ONE AT A TIME, DOES NOT COME EASILY.

BUT WHEN ACQUIRED IT CAN BE EXECUTED WITH WONDERFUL FACILITY AND SPEED, AND THE RUSE IS PRACTICALLY UNDETECTABLE.

THE SHUFFLE MAY BE CONTINUED TO ANY LENGTH BY UNDER-CUTTING BELOW THE STOCK, JOGGING THE FIRST CARD, SHUFFLING OFF AND THEN AGAIN UNDER-CUTTING TO JOG AND THROWING ON TOP;

OR THE BLIND TOP STOCK, APPARENT SHUFFLE OF THE WHOLE DECK, MAY BE MADE AS DESCRIBED IN THIS WORK.

TWO OR MORE HANDS MAY BE RUN UP BY THIS METHOD, IF ONE SET IS PLACED AT THE TOP AND THE OTHER AT THE BOTTOM.

THE PROCESS IS TO FIRST DRAW FROM THE TOP, THEN FROM THE BOTTOM, IN SUCCESSION, UNTIL ALL THE SELECTED CARDS HAVE BEEN ARRANGED ALTERNATELY AT THE BOTTOM OF THE LEFT-HAND PACKET, THEN SHUFFLE OFF BALANCE.

THEN RUN SEVERAL CARDS FROM THE TOP FOR A START, AND THEN DRAW THE FIRST CARD FROM THE BOTTOM.

THEN RUN FROM THE TOP THE NUMBER THAT THERE ARE PLAYERS BETWEEN WHERE THE FIRST BOTTOM CARD IS TO FALL, AND WHERE THE SECOND ONE IS INTENDED.

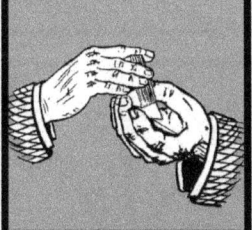
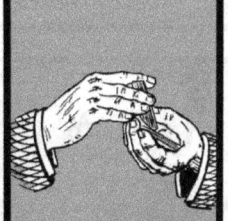
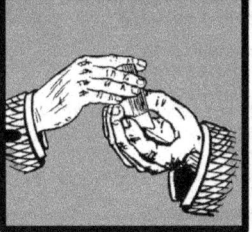

THEN DRAW AGAIN FROM THE BOTTOM, AND SO ON UNTIL THE TWO SETS HAVE BEEN RUN UP.

THE CALCULATION IS VERY SIMPLE AND OF COURSE SHOULD BE MADE BEFOREHAND.

FOR INSTANCE, IN A FIVE-HANDED GAME OF POKER ASSUME THAT THREE QUEENS AND THREE NINES ARE TO BE STOCKED.

THE QUEENS ARE TO GO TO THE MAN WHO CUTS, AND THE NINES TO THE SECOND PLAYER FROM THE DEALER.

PLACE THE QUEENS ON TOP, THE NINES UNDER.

RUN QUEEN, THEN DRAW A NINE, AND SO ON UNTIL ALL ARE UNDER THE DECK.

THEN THE CALCULATION WOULD BE, ON EVERY FIVE CARDS THAT ARE SHUFFLED, TO DRAW THE SECOND AND FOURTH FROM THE BOTTOM.

THE CARDS MUST BE RUN UP IN THE REVERSE ORDER, SO THE COUNT IS MADE TO THE RIGHT, THE DEALER BEING FIRST. HIS CARD COMES FROM THE TOP.

THEN THE SECOND CARD FROM THE BOTTOM, WHICH IS THE QUEEN,

THEN THE THIRD FROM THE TOP, THEN THE FOURTH FROM THE BOTTOM, WHICH IS THE NINE, THEN THE FIFTH AND FIRST AGAIN FROM THE TOP, THEN THE SECOND FROM THE BOTTOM, AND SO ON UNTIL FIFTEEN CARDS HAVE BEEN RUN.

THEN OUT-JOG AND SHUFFLE OFF. THEN UNDER-CUT TO JOG AND THROW ON TOP.

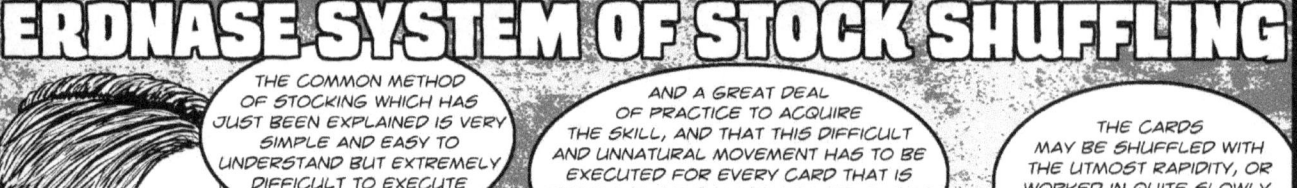

ERDNASE SYSTEM OF STOCK SHUFFLING

THE COMMON METHOD OF STOCKING WHICH HAS JUST BEEN EXPLAINED IS VERY SIMPLE AND EASY TO UNDERSTAND BUT EXTREMELY DIFFICULT TO EXECUTE PERFECTLY.

THE PRINCIPAL OBJECTIONS ARE THAT DRAWING FROM THE BOTTOM IS AN UNNATURAL MOVEMENT, THAT IT REQUIRES MUCH SKILL TO ACCOMPLISH THE FEAT GRACEFULLY,

AND A GREAT DEAL OF PRACTICE TO ACQUIRE THE SKILL, AND THAT THIS DIFFICULT AND UNNATURAL MOVEMENT HAS TO BE EXECUTED FOR EVERY CARD THAT IS PUT IN THE STOCK, THEREBY INCREASING THE CHANCES OF ATTRACTING ATTENTION WHEN THE STOCK IS LARGE.

THE NEW METHOD ABOUT TO BE DESCRIBED IS INFINITELY EASIER OF EXECUTION, AND THE MOVEMENTS ARE SO NATURAL AND REGULAR THAT A VERY INDIFFERENT PERFORMER CAN DEFY THE CLOSEST SCRUTINY.

THE CARDS MAY BE SHUFFLED WITH THE UTMOST RAPIDITY, OR WORKED IN QUITE SLOWLY, WITHOUT FEAR OF EXPOSING THE ACTION.

THE TIME REQUIRED IS NOT GREATER THAN USUALLY TAKEN IN AN ORDINARY SHUFFLE, AND THE CALCULATIONS ARE SIMPLE.

THE PRINCIPAL AIDS IN THIS NEW METHOD ARE THE JOGS AND THE BREAK, AND THEY ARE USED TO HOLD AND SEPARATE AND LOCATE SOLELY BY THE SENSE OF TOUCH, THE VARIOUS DIVISIONS CREATED DURING THE SHUFFLE.

THE ENTIRE STOCK IS RUN UP INDEPENDENT OF SIGHT, AND, IN FACT, THE DEALER CAN NO MORE FOLLOW THE ACTION WITH HIS EYES THAN CAN THOSE WHO ARE MOST INTERESTED IN SCRUTINIZING HIS WORK.

WE WILL GIVE AS A FIRST ILLUSTRATION THE ACTION REQUIRED FOR STOCKING TWO CARDS IN ANY GAME THAT IS DEALT ONE CARD AT A TIME TO EACH PLAYER.

THE POSITION GIVEN FOR SHUFFLING MUST BE MAINTAINED.

TWO-CARD STOCK

THE TWO DESIRED CARDS ARE PLACED ON TOP, UNDER-CUT ABOUT HALF THE DECK, IN-JOG TOP CARD, RUN TWO LESS THAN TWICE THE NUMBER OF PLAYERS, OUT-JOG AND SHUFFLE OFF.

UNDER-CUT TO OUT-JOG, FORMING BREAK AT IN-JOG; RUN ONE LESS THAN NUMBER OF PLAYERS, IN-JOG AND SHUFFLE OFF. UNDER-CUT TO IN-JOG AND THROW ON TOP.

THIS ACTION PLACES THE TWO DESIRED CARDS SO THAT THEY WILL FALL TO THE DEALER IN THE FIRST TWO ROUNDS.

Five-Card Stock

For any game in which cards are dealt singly.

Four desired cards on top, one on bottom. Under-cut about one-third deck, in-jog top card, run two less than twice number players, out-jog and shuffle last card on top.

Under-cut to out-jog, forming break at in-jog; run one less than number players, throw to break, run two, in-jog one and shuffle off.

Under-cut to in-jog and throw on top.

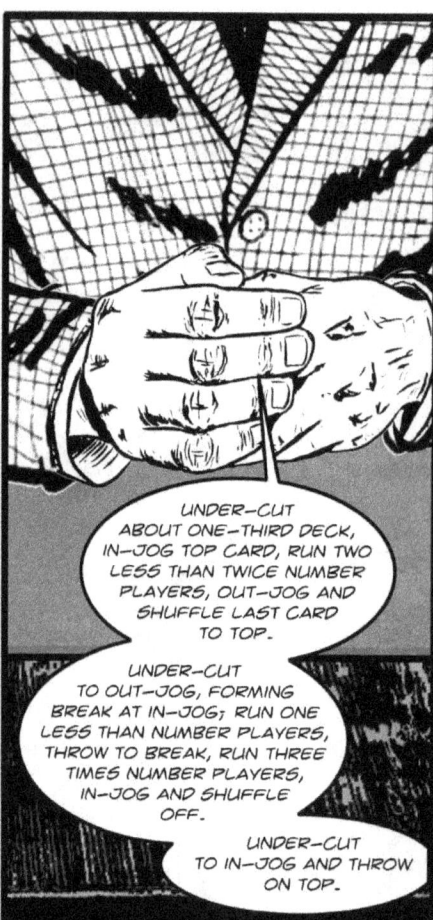

Under-cut about one-third deck, in-jog top card, run two less than twice number players, out-jog and shuffle last card to top.

Under-cut to out-jog, forming break at in-jog; run one less than number players, throw to break, run three times number players, in-jog and shuffle off.

Under-cut to in-jog and throw on top.

This gives the dealer the five cards in five rounds.

The formula appears long, but much of the shuffle is a repetition, very simple, and takes but a second or two longer than the four-card stock.

To show the possibilities of this method, we give a fancy stock for a game of poker that will throw four of a kind to the dealer and leave two sets of fours on the top for the draw.

Twelve-Card Stock

For draw poker.

Three sets of fours on top, the set for the dealer to be the under-most.

Take whole deck in right hand, run nine and throw balance on top, forming in-jog with throw.

Undercut about one-third deck, forming break at in-jog, in-jog top card, run two less than twice number players, out-jog, shuffle off to break and throw on top.

Undercut to out-jog, forming break at in-jog, run one less than number players, throw to break, run one, in-jog running one less than three times number players, out-jog and shuffle off.

Under-cut to in-jog and throw on top. Under-cut to out-jog, run one less than number players and throw on top.

This gives the dealer the first of his set of four on the second round, and leaves the other two sets on top for the draw.

If the dealer's set is the highest of the three it matters little to him how the draw is made, as none of the players can get a better hand even by drawing four.

Euchre Stock

Four-handed game.

Four desired cards on top. Under-cut about three-quarters of deck, run seventeen, in-jog and shuffle off.

Under-cut to in-jog and throw on top.

This will give three of the desired cards to the dealer and turn the fourth for trump.

The dealer takes two cards the first round and three on the last, thereby getting three of the desired cards on the last round and turning the fourth for trump.

The calculation is in merely counting the number of cards required in the deal before reaching the desired cards, which are for the dealer and the trump.

In a three-handed game the run would be twelve—i. e., five less.

In a two-handed game, seven. As described above, the shuffle is too short.

A blind shuffle should be first executed, leaving the desired cards on top, and then the stock run up.

If the two bowers are among the desired cards the left must not be turned for trumps, so it may be placed at any position among the desired cards save the under one.

If the desired cards are to be given to the dealer's partner the action is almost as short.

Euchre Stock

Four-handed game. Four desired cards on top for partner and trump.

Under-cut about three-quarters of deck, in-jog top card, run sixteen, out-jog and shuffle off.

Under-cut to out-jog, forming break at in-jog, in-jog first card running eleven, throw to break, run three and shuffle off.

Under-cut to in-jog and shuffle off.

This gives the player opposite the dealer three of the desired cards on the second round, and turns the fourth card for trumps.

ERDNASE SYSTEM OF CULL SHUFFLING

IN MOST CARD GAMES WHERE THERE IS A STAKE AT ISSUE THE SCRUTINY IS SO CLOSE AND THE RULES ARE SO STRICT, THAT THE EXPERT CARD HANDLER FINDS LITTLE OPPORTUNITY TO MAKE AN OPEN SELECTION OF ANY PARTICULAR CARDS.

THE SLIGHTEST ACTION THAT INDICATES SUCH A PURPOSE INVITES SUSPICION, AND THERE IS AN OLD ADAGE MUCH QUOTED THAT RUNS, "IF SUSPECTED, QUIT."

HOWEVER, WE SHALL DESCRIBE A NEW METHOD OF MAKING MANY SELECTIONS WITHOUT A POSSIBILITY OF THE DESIGN BEING DETECTED, AND IN A MANNER SO NATURAL AND REGULAR THAT NOT A MOVEMENT IS MADE THAT INDICATES ANYTHING MORE THAN THE PURPOSE OF THOROUGHLY SHUFFLING THE DECK.

THE NECESSARY PREPARATION FOR THE CULL SHUFFLE IS TO NOTE AT WHAT PARTICULAR NUMBER THE FIRST OF THE DESIRED CARDS WILL STAND FROM THE TOP WHEN THROWN ON THE DECK, AND AT WHAT NUMBER THE NEXT WILL STAND FROM THE FIRST, AND SO ON FOR AS MANY CARDS AS ARE TO BE CULLED.

FOR INSTANCE, IF THERE ARE THREE DESIRED CARDS, THE FIRST THE EIGHTH FROM THE TOP, THE NEXT THE FOURTH FROM THAT, AND THE NEXT THE SIXTH CARD FURTHER DOWN, THEIR ORDER IS FIXED IN THE MIND AS EIGHT, FOUR, SIX.

THE LOWEST DESIRED CARD IS EIGHTEENTH CARD FROM THE TOP OF THE DECK, BUT THE COUNT IS MADE FROM ONE DESIRED CARD TO THE OTHER.

IF THE DESIRED CARDS WERE TOGETHER, THE FIRST ONE THE EIGHTH FROM THE TOP, AND THE OTHERS THE NEXT TWO CARDS, THE COUNT WOULD STAND EIGHT, ONE, ONE.

THE CALCULATION OF THE POSITIONS THE CARDS WILL TAKE WHEN THROWN ON THE DECK IS MADE BEFORE THE DEALER GATHERS THEM UP TO SHUFFLE, OR, AS HE IS DOING SO.

IT IS A VERY SIMPLE MATTER TO NOTE THE ORDER IN WHICH TWO OR THREE DESIRABLE CARDS LIE, OR, FOR THAT MATTER, FIVE OR SIX.

IN SOME GAMES THE NOTE IS MADE AS THE TRICKS ARE TAKEN.

IN OTHERS THE LAST CARDS THAT ARE FACED ON THE TABLE GIVE SUFFICIENT CHOICE.

FOR INSTANCE, IF TWO HANDS ARE SHOWN IN A POKER GAME, ONE HOLDING A SMALL PAIR AND THE OTHER A SIDE CARD TO MATCH THE PAIR, A GLANCE WOULD DETERMINE THE ORDER THE THREE OF A KIND WOULD TAKE WHEN THROWN ON THE DECK. OF COURSE, IT WOULD NOT DO TO MAKE UP THE DESIRED CARDS FROM ONE HAND.

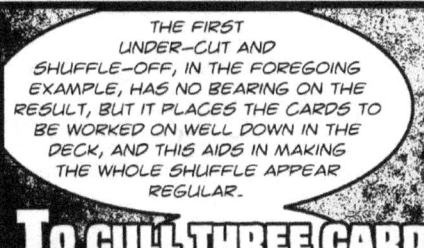

IT IS NECESSARY TO PUT SOME LITTLE BRAINS INTO SO SIMPLE A PROBLEM AS ADDING TWO AND TWO TOGETHER, AND TO BECOME ACCOMPLISHED AT CULLING ONE MUST HAVE AN UNDERSTANDING OF THE **CAUSE AND EFFECT** OF THE VARIOUS ACTIONS.

IT IS IMPOSSIBLE TO GIVE A FORMULA THAT WILL ANSWER FOR EVERY SITUATION.

THERE IS NO END TO THE VARIETY OF POSITIONS THE DESIRED CARDS MAY BE IN.

BUT WITH A THOROUGH KNOWLEDGE OF THE TWO EXAMPLES GIVEN, AND THE REASON FOR EACH PARTICULAR ACTION, THE STUDENT WILL BE FAIRLY ESTABLISHED ON THE ROAD TO SUCCESS, AND HAVE OVERCOME BY FAR THE GREATEST DIFFICULTY.

TO CULL FOUR CARDS, NUMBERS 3, 6, 2, 5.

UNDER-CUT ABOUT ONE-THIRD DECK, IN-JOG FIRST CARD AND SHUFFLE OFF. UNDER-CUT TO IN-JOG, RUN ONE LESS THAN FIRST NUMBER, IN-JOG RUNNING ONE MORE THAN SECOND NUMBER, OUT-JOG RUNNING ONE LESS THAN THIRD NUMBER, AND THROW ON TOP.

(TWO OF THE CARDS ARE NOW AT TOP AND BOTTOM OF MIDDLE PACKET, ONE ON TOP OF DECK, AND THE LAST AT ITS ORIGINAL NUMBER FROM TOP CARD.)

UNDER-CUT TO OUT-JOG, FORMING BREAK AT IN-JOG, IN-JOG TOP CARD, RUN ONE, THROW TO BREAK AND SHUFFLE OFF. (THREE CARDS ARE NOW TOGETHER AT IN-JOG, AND LAST CARD AT ITS NUMBER BELOW IN-JOG.)

UNDER-CUT TO IN-JOG AND RUN ONE LESS THAN LAST NUMBER AND THROW ON TOP. (THREE OF THE CARDS ARE NOW AT THE BOTTOM, THE FOURTH ON TOP.)

THE TOP CARD CAN NOW BE BROUGHT TO THE BOTTOM WITH ITS FELLOWS BY AN UNDER-CUT TO TOP CARD AND A THROW ON TOP; OR, UNDER-CUT ABOUT HALF DECK, IN-JOG TOP CARD, AND THROW ON TOP; THEN UNDER-CUT TO IN-JOG AND SHUFFLE OFF.

TO UNDER-CUT TO TOP CARD AND THROW ON TOP, OR, IN OTHER WORDS, TO RUN ONE AND THROW BALANCE ON TOP, IF DONE RAPIDLY, APPEARS LIKE A SIMPLE CUT, AND THE FACT THAT BUT ONE CARD IS TAKEN FROM THE TOP TO THE BOTTOM CANNOT BE DETECTED.

THESE EXAMPLES OF CULLING, IF FAIRLY WELL EXECUTED, HAVE ALL THE APPEARANCE OF AN ORDINARY SHUFFLE, AND WHEN PERFORMED WITH THE SMOOTHNESS AND GRACE OF A CLEVER CARD HANDLER IT IS ABSOLUTELY IMPOSSIBLE TO DETECT THE LEAST MANIPULATION.

IT WILL BE NOTICED IN THE EXAMPLES GIVEN THAT CULLING IS LARGELY A REPETITION OF THE SAME ACTIONS, AS THE NUMBER TO BE CULLED INCREASES; AND CONSEQUENTLY THE TIME REQUIRED IS GREATER.

BUT SHOULD THE DESIRED CARDS RUN TOGETHER IN PAIRS, AS THREES OR MORE, THE ACTION AND TIME ARE SHORTENED PROPORTIONATELY. SETS OF CARDS RUNNING TOGETHER ARE TREATED MUCH AS THOUGH EACH SET WERE ONE CARD.

IF THE ORDER BE 6, 1, 1, 1, 4, 1, 1, THE ACTION OF GETTING THEM ALL TOGETHER WILL BE MUCH THE SAME AS THOUGH THEY WERE BUT TWO CARDS AT 6, 4.

IF THE ORDER WERE 5, 1, 1, 1, 3, 1, 1, 7, 1, THE ACTION WOULD BE ABOUT THE SAME AS A THREE-CARD CULL SHUFFLE, THOUGH THERE ARE NINE DESIRED CARDS ACTUALLY RUN DOWN TO THE BOTTOM.

TO CULL NINE CARDS, NUMBERS 5, 1, 1, 1, 3, 1, 1, 7, 1.

UNDER-CUT ABOUT ONE-THIRD DECK, IN-JOG FIRST CARD AND SHUFFLE OFF.

UNDER-CUT TO IN-JOG AND RUN ONE LESS THAN FIRST NUMBER, IN-JOG RUNNING ALL CARDS TO AND INCLUDING LAST CARD OF SECOND SET. (THIS RUN IS NINE, FOUR IN FIRST SET, TWO INDIFFERENT CARDS, THREE IN SECOND SET.)

OUT-JOG RUNNING ONE LESS THAN NEXT NUMBER (SIX), AND THROW ON TOP. (THIS PLACES FIRST TWO SETS AT TOP AND BOTTOM OF MIDDLE PACKET, AND THIRD SET ON TOP.)

UNDER-CUT TO OUT-JOG, FORMING BREAK AT IN-JOG, IN-JOG TOP CARD, RUN SECOND SET (THREE), THROW TO BREAK AND SHUFFLE OFF.

(ALL THE DESIRED CARDS ARE NOW TOGETHER, BUT THE IN-JOG DIVIDES THE LAST TWO.)

UNDER-CUT TO IN-JOG AND THROW ON TOP. THIS LEAVES ONE CARD ON TOP AND EIGHT ON BOTTOM.

THIS EXAMPLE MIGHT WELL BE TERMED A FANCY CULL, AS RUNNING DOWN SO MANY CARDS WILL RARELY BE ATTEMPTED, BUT IT SHOWS THE POSSIBILITIES OF THE SYSTEM.

BEFORE THE SHUFFLE IS BEGUN THE ENTIRE ACTION SHOULD BE MENTALLY REHEARSED SO THAT THERE WILL BE **NO HESITATION** IN THE PROCEDURE.

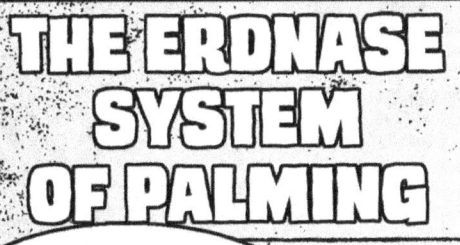

THE ERDNASE SYSTEM OF PALMING

THE ART OF CARD PALMING CAN BE BROUGHT TO A DEGREE OF PERFECTION THAT BORDERS ON THE WONDERFUL.

IT IS VERY SIMPLE TO PLACE ONE OR SEVERAL CARDS IN THE PALM AND CONCEAL THEM BY PARTLY CLOSING AND TURNING THE PALM DOWNWARD, OR INWARD; BUT IT IS ENTIRELY ANOTHER MATTER TO PALM THEM FROM THE DECK IN SUCH A MANNER THAT THE MOST CRITICAL OBSERVER WOULD NOT EVEN SUSPECT, LET ALONE DETECT, THE ACTION.

THE METHODS FOLLOWING WERE ORIGINATED BY US, AND WE BELIEVE THEM TO BE THE MOST RAPID AND SUBTLE EVER DEVISED.

TO PALM, PRESS THE RIGHT LITTLE FINGER, EXACTLY AT THE FIRST JOINT, FIRMLY AGAINST THE TOP CARDS, PULL THEM UP ABOUT HALF AN INCH AT CORNER, FREEING THEM FROM THE LEFT SECOND AND THIRD FINGERS, KEEPING THE THREE RIGHT FINGERS (LITTLE, SECOND AND THIRD) PERFECTLY STRAIGHT.

THE CARDS TO BE PALMED ARE NOW HELD FIRMLY BETWEEN THE RIGHT LITTLE FINGER, AND THE LEFT LITTLE FINGER. (SEE FIG. 36.)

Fig. 36

STRAIGHTEN OUT RIGHT FIRST FINGER, SWING LEFT LITTLE FINGER WITH THE CARDS TO BE PALMED FREE OF THE END OF THE DECK, PRESS THE CARDS INTO THE RIGHT PALM WITH THE END OF THE LEFT THIRD FINGER. (SEE FIG. 37.)

Fig. 37

 TOP PALM. FIRST METHOD

HOLD THE DECK IN THE LEFT HAND SO THAT THE FIRST JOINTS OF THE SECOND AND THIRD FINGERS WILL BE AGAINST THE MIDDLE OF ONE SIDE, THE THUMB AGAINST MIDDLE OF OPPOSITE SIDE, THE FIRST JOINT OF LITTLE FINGER AGAINST MIDDLE OF END AND FIRST FINGER CURLED UP AGAINST BOTTOM.

BRING THE RIGHT HAND OVER TOP OF DECK, THE THIRD, SECOND AND LITTLE FINGERS CLOSE TOGETHER, FIRST JOINT OF THE LITTLE FINGER BEING AGAINST THE END CORNER, THE FIRST FINGER CURLED UP ON TOP AND THE TIP OF THUMB RESTING IDLY AT END, ABOVE LEFT LITTLE FINGER.

Fig. 38

DRAW THE DECK OUT ABOUT HALF WAY FROM UNDER THE RIGHT HAND, AND RELEASE THE LEFT HAND ENTIRELY. (SEE FIG. 38.)

THEN THE RIGHT DROPS THE DECK ON THE TABLE TO BE CUT.

AFTER THE HANDS ARE IN THE FIRST POSITION THE WHOLE PROCESS DOES NOT OCCUPY HALF A SECOND.

THE ACTION OF DRAWING THE DECK INTO VIEW WHEN THE CARDS ARE PALMED IS MADE A PART OF THE WHOLE MOVEMENT.

THE DECK SHOULD BE KEPT IN VIEW AS MUCH AS POSSIBLE, AND THE RIGHT FIRST FINGER IS CURLED UP ON TOP FOR THAT PURPOSE UNTIL THE INSTANT THE PALM IS PERFORMED.

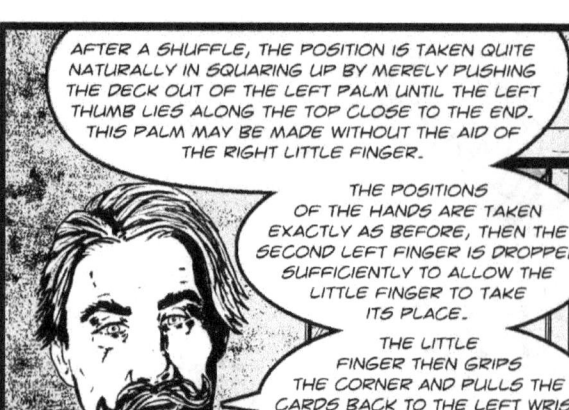

After a shuffle, the position is taken quite naturally in squaring up by merely pushing the deck out of the left palm until the left thumb lies along the top close to the end. This palm may be made without the aid of the right little finger.

The positions of the hands are taken exactly as before, then the second left finger is dropped sufficiently to allow the little finger to take its place.

The little finger then grips the corner and pulls the cards back to the left wrist until they lie along the left fingers as before.

Bottom Palm. Second Method.

Seize the deck with the right hand on top, by the middle of the ends between the thumb and first joints of second and third fingers, first finger curled up on top.

Bring the left hand up against the bottom, the left second and third finger tips resting idly on the right second and third fingers,

The left little finger at first joint against the edge of the bottom cards at the same end, the left first finger curled up against bottom and the left thumb resting against the side.

Fig. 41

To palm, grip the corner of the under cards with the left little finger at first joint. (See Fig. 41.)

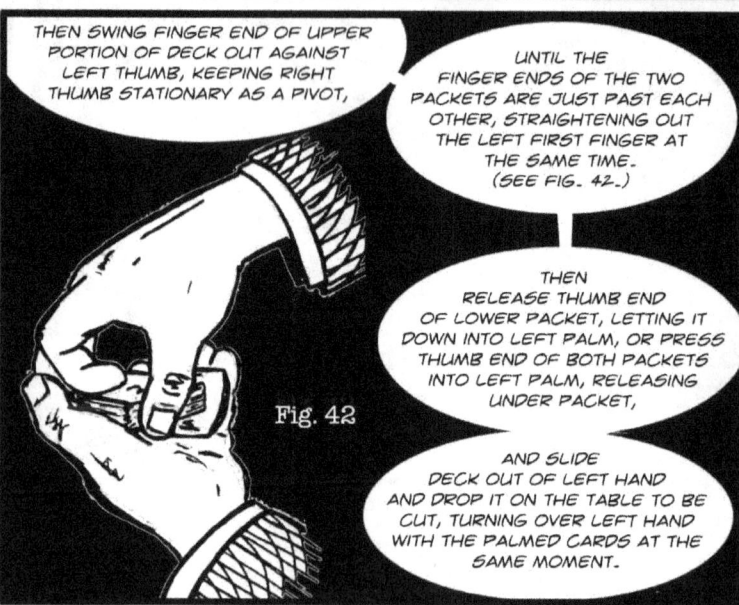

Then swing finger end of upper portion of deck out against left thumb, keeping right thumb stationary as a pivot,

Until the finger ends of the two packets are just past each other, straightening out the left first finger at the same time. (See Fig. 42.)

Fig. 42

Then release thumb end of lower packet, letting it down into left palm, or press thumb end of both packets into left palm, releasing under packet,

And slide deck out of left hand and drop it on the table to be cut, turning over left hand with the palmed cards at the same moment.

The whole process is as quick as a flash, and quite imperceptible.

The drawback is the slightly unnatural action of bringing the left fingers to the end of the deck.

They should be kept at the side in squaring up after the shuffle, then at the last instant slipped to the end, and without a moment's hesitation the palm is made.

To replace the bottom palm, pick up the deck by the ends with the right hand, and as it is placed in the left slide the left second finger from the end of the palmed cards to the side, curl the left first finger up underneath (see Fig. 43),

Fig. 43

And as the palmed cards are slipped into position bring the left thumb against one side and the left second finger to the other, which materially aid in the rotary movement of the under packet.

It is more difficult to replace than to palm, but the action is not so liable to attract attention, as, if the palm is not suspected, any awkwardness at replacing may be covered by squaring up the cut.

But replacing may be performed just as perfectly as palming, and to become proficient in either requires some practice. When the positions and process are thoroughly understood the main difficulties are overcome.

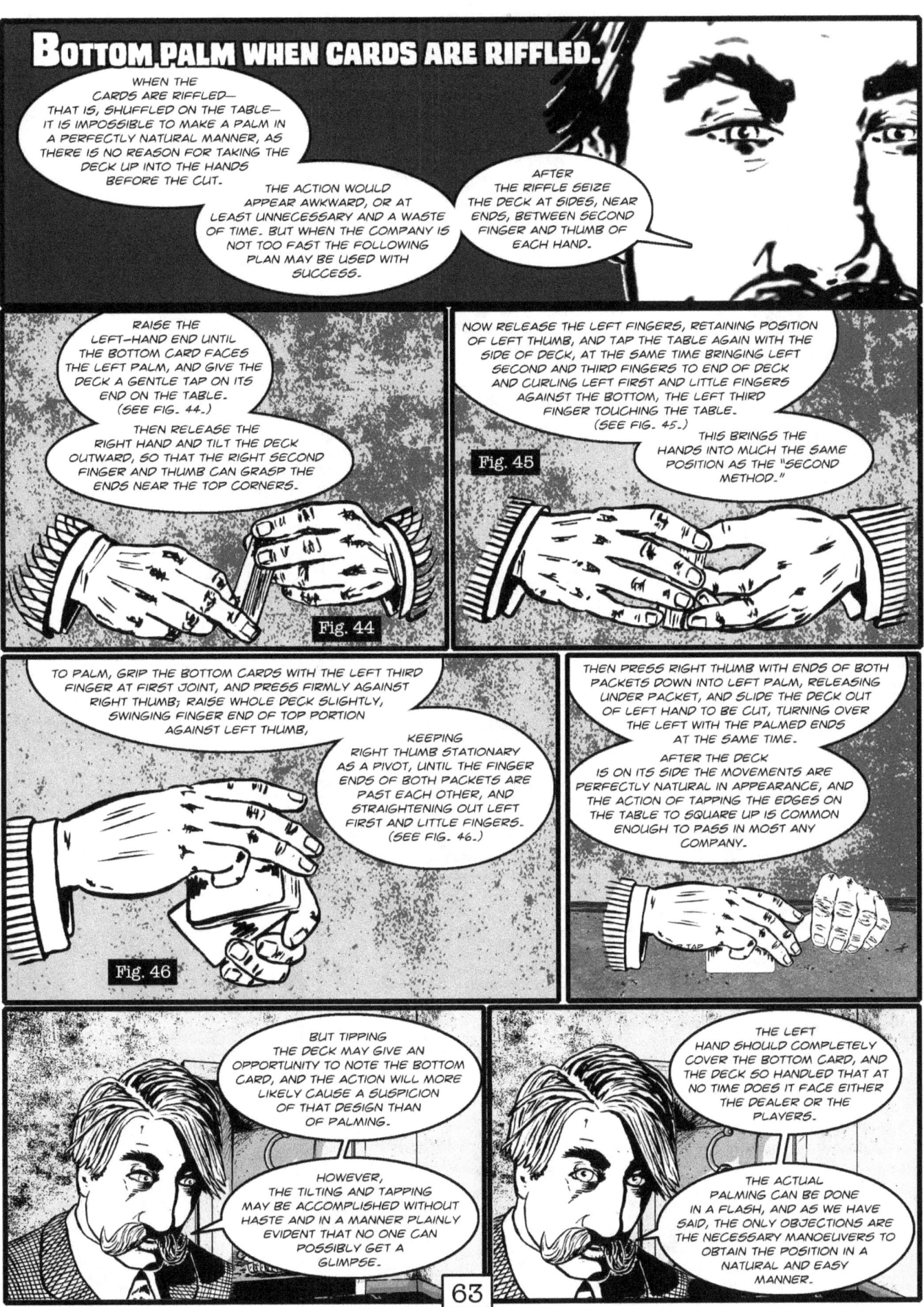

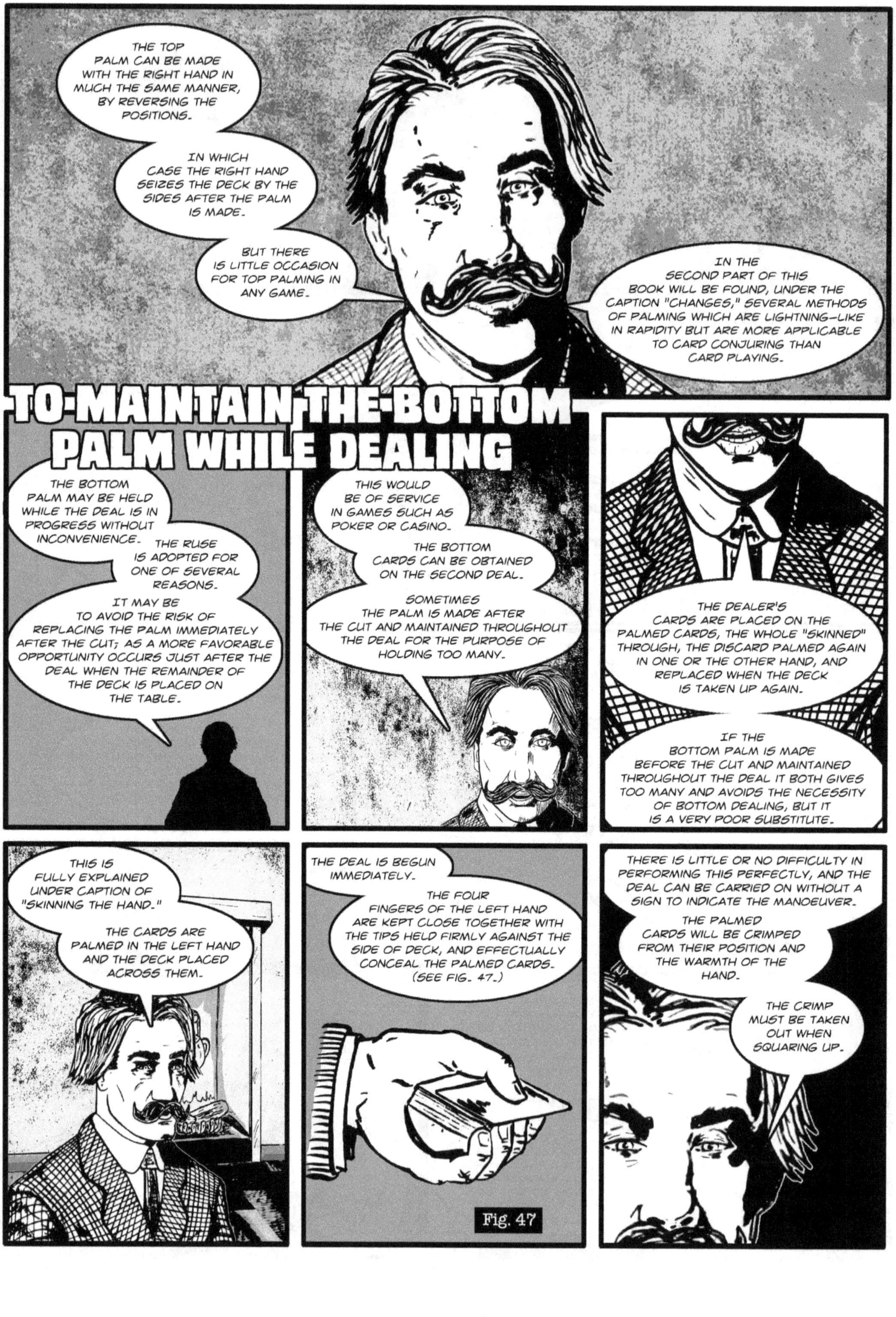

THE TOP PALM CAN BE MADE WITH THE RIGHT HAND IN MUCH THE SAME MANNER, BY REVERSING THE POSITIONS.

IN WHICH CASE THE RIGHT HAND SEIZES THE DECK BY THE SIDES AFTER THE PALM IS MADE.

BUT THERE IS LITTLE OCCASION FOR TOP PALMING IN ANY GAME.

IN THE SECOND PART OF THIS BOOK WILL BE FOUND, UNDER THE CAPTION "CHANGES," SEVERAL METHODS OF PALMING WHICH ARE LIGHTNING-LIKE IN RAPIDITY BUT ARE MORE APPLICABLE TO CARD CONJURING THAN CARD PLAYING.

TO MAINTAIN THE BOTTOM PALM WHILE DEALING

THE BOTTOM PALM MAY BE HELD WHILE THE DEAL IS IN PROGRESS WITHOUT INCONVENIENCE. THE RUSE IS ADOPTED FOR ONE OF SEVERAL REASONS.

IT MAY BE TO AVOID THE RISK OF REPLACING THE PALM IMMEDIATELY AFTER THE CUT; AS A MORE FAVORABLE OPPORTUNITY OCCURS JUST AFTER THE DEAL WHEN THE REMAINDER OF THE DECK IS PLACED ON THE TABLE.

THIS WOULD BE OF SERVICE IN GAMES SUCH AS POKER OR CASINO.

THE BOTTOM CARDS CAN BE OBTAINED ON THE SECOND DEAL.

SOMETIMES THE PALM IS MADE AFTER THE CUT AND MAINTAINED THROUGHOUT THE DEAL FOR THE PURPOSE OF HOLDING TOO MANY.

THE DEALER'S CARDS ARE PLACED ON THE PALMED CARDS, THE WHOLE "SKINNED" THROUGH, THE DISCARD PALMED AGAIN IN ONE OR THE OTHER HAND, AND REPLACED WHEN THE DECK IS TAKEN UP AGAIN.

IF THE BOTTOM PALM IS MADE BEFORE THE CUT AND MAINTAINED THROUGHOUT THE DEAL IT BOTH GIVES TOO MANY AND AVOIDS THE NECESSITY OF BOTTOM DEALING, BUT IT IS A VERY POOR SUBSTITUTE.

THIS IS FULLY EXPLAINED UNDER CAPTION OF "SKINNING THE HAND."

THE CARDS ARE PALMED IN THE LEFT HAND AND THE DECK PLACED ACROSS THEM.

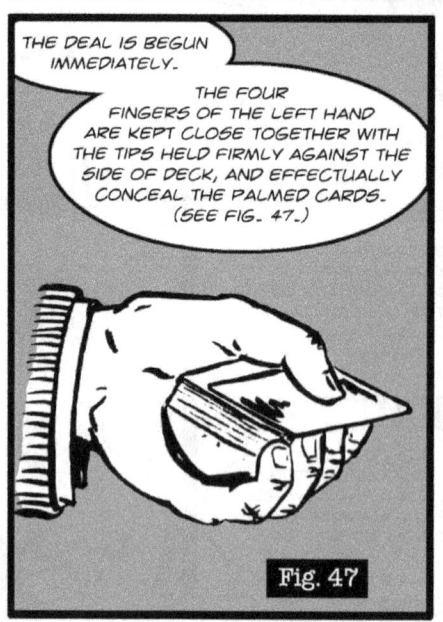

THE DEAL IS BEGUN IMMEDIATELY.

THE FOUR FINGERS OF THE LEFT HAND ARE KEPT CLOSE TOGETHER WITH THE TIPS HELD FIRMLY AGAINST THE SIDE OF DECK, AND EFFECTUALLY CONCEAL THE PALMED CARDS. (SEE FIG. 47.)

Fig. 47

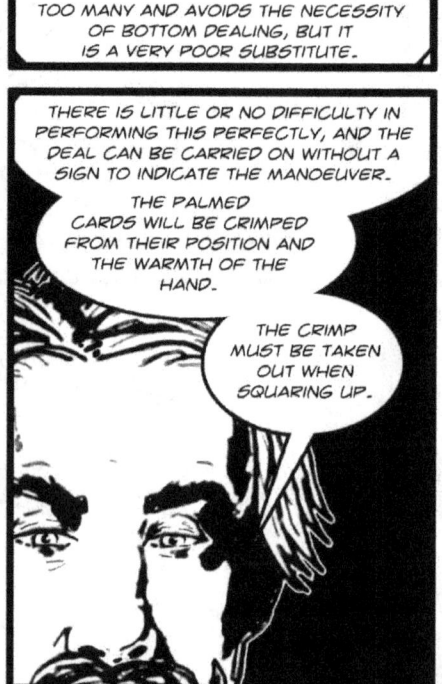

THERE IS LITTLE OR NO DIFFICULTY IN PERFORMING THIS PERFECTLY, AND THE DEAL CAN BE CARRIED ON WITHOUT A SIGN TO INDICATE THE MANOEUVER.

THE PALMED CARDS WILL BE CRIMPED FROM THEIR POSITION AND THE WARMTH OF THE HAND.

THE CRIMP MUST BE TAKEN OUT WHEN SQUARING UP.

TO HOLD THE LOCATION OF CUT WHILE DEALING

THE OBJECT OF HOLDING THE LOCATION OF THE CUT IS SO THAT A SHIFT MAY BE MADE AT THAT POINT WHEN THE FIRST DEAL HAS BEEN COMPLETED.

THIS WILL BRING THE ORIGINAL BOTTOM CARDS TO THAT POSITION AGAIN, FROM WHICH THEY MAY BE DEALT DURING THE SECOND DEAL, AND THE MOST OPPORTUNE MOMENT FOR THE SHIFT IS IMMEDIATELY AFTER THE FIRST DEAL, AS THE DECK IS DEPOSITED ON THE TABLE.

WHEN THE CUT IS MADE, PICK UP THE PACKET THAT WAS UNDER, BY THE SIDES, NEAR END, BETWEEN SECOND AND THIRD FINGERS AND THUMB OF RIGHT HAND, AND LAY IT ON TOP OF PACKET CUT-OFF, SO THAT THE THEN UNDER PACKET FORMS A JOG OR PROTRUDES ABOUT QUARTER OF AN INCH TOWARD THE RIGHT WRIST.

PICK UP THE TWO PACKETS THE INSTANT THE ONE IS PLACED ON THE OTHER, BY A SLIDING MOVEMENT, WITH THE FINGERS IN THE SAME POSITION, AND PLACE THE DECK ACROSS THE LEFT PALM WITH THE LEFT THUMB ON TOP TO HOLD IT IN POSITION.

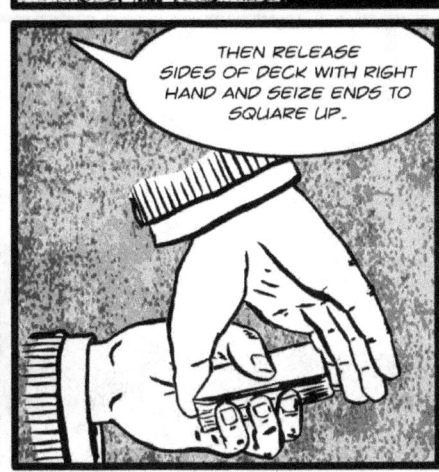

THEN RELEASE SIDES OF DECK WITH RIGHT HAND AND SEIZE ENDS TO SQUARE UP.

IN DOING SO THE RIGHT THUMB COMES AGAINST THE INNER END AND IN CONTACT WITH THE JOG OR PROJECTING UNDER PACKET.

PRESS THIS DOWN A LITTLE WITH THE THUMB AND SQUARE ENDS OF DECK, FORMING BREAK AT THUMB END.

NOW SHIFT THE LEFT HAND SLIGHTLY SO AS TO HOLD THE BREAK WITH THE TIP OF THE LEFT LITTLE FINGER AT THE SIDE, CLOSE TO THE END, AND BEGIN THE DEAL. (SEE FIG. 48.)

Fig. 48.

THE BREAK IS NOT MORE THAN AN EIGHTH OF AN INCH WIDE, AND IS CONCEALED BY THE LEFT THIRD FINGER.

THE ACTION IS VERY SIMPLE, YET SHOULD BE CAREFULLY STUDIED.

THE SLIGHT JOG IN THE TWO PACKETS AS THEY ARE PICKED UP IS NOT NOTICEABLE, AS THE TOP PACKET OVERHANGS AT THE OUTER END AND THE ONE MOST LIKELY TO SHOW IS HIDDEN BY THE RIGHT HAND.

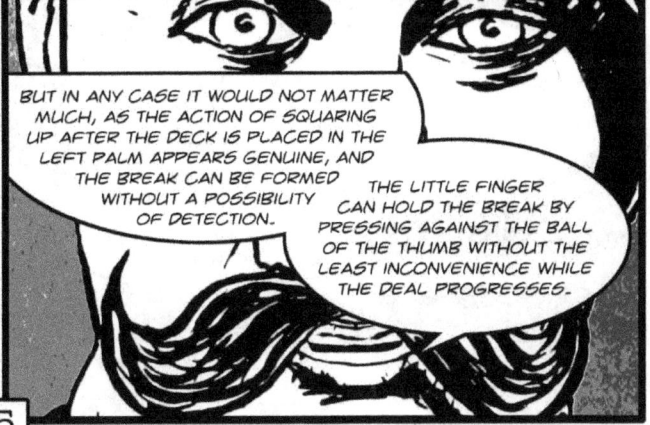

BUT IN ANY CASE IT WOULD NOT MATTER MUCH, AS THE ACTION OF SQUARING UP AFTER THE DECK IS PLACED IN THE LEFT PALM APPEARS GENUINE, AND THE BREAK CAN BE FORMED WITHOUT A POSSIBILITY OF DETECTION. THE LITTLE FINGER CAN HOLD THE BREAK BY PRESSING AGAINST THE BALL OF THE THUMB WITHOUT THE LEAST INCONVENIENCE WHILE THE DEAL PROGRESSES.

SHIFTS

THERE ARE MANY METHODS OF PERFORMING THE MANOEUVER THAT REVERSES THE ACTION OF THE CUT, BUT IN THIS PART OF OUR WORK WE WILL DESCRIBE BUT THREE WHICH WE CONSIDER AT ALL PRACTICABLE AT THE CARD TABLE.

THIS ARTIFICE IS ERRONEOUSLY SUPPOSED TO BE INDISPENSABLE TO THE PROFESSIONAL PLAYER, BUT THE TRUTH IS IT IS LITTLE USED, AND ADOPTED ONLY AS A LAST RESORT.

THE CONJURER EMPLOYS THE SHIFT IN NINE-TENTHS OF HIS CARD TRICKS, AND UNDER HIS ENVIRONMENTS IT IS COMPARATIVELY VERY SIMPLE TO PERFORM.

A HALF TURN OF THE BODY, OR A SLIGHT SWING OF THE HANDS, OR THE USE OF "PATTER" UNTIL A FAVORABLE MOMENT OCCURS, ENABLES HIM TO COVER THE ACTION PERFECTLY.

BUT SEATED AT THE CARD TABLE IN A MONEY GAME, THE CONDITIONS ARE DIFFERENT.

THE HANDS MAY NOT BE WITHDRAWN FROM THE TABLE FOR AN INSTANT, AND ANY UNUSUAL SWING OR TURN WILL NOT BE TOLERATED,

AND A STILL GREATER HANDICAP ARISES FROM THE FACT THAT THE OBJECT OF A SHIFT IS WELL KNOWN, AND ESPECIALLY THE EXACT MOMENT TO EXPECT IT, IMMEDIATELY AFTER THE CUT.

THE SHIFT HAS YET TO BE INVENTED THAT CAN BE EXECUTED BY A MOVEMENT APPEARING AS COINCIDENT CARD-TABLE ROUTINE;

OR THAT CAN BE EXECUTED WITH THE HANDS HELD STATIONARY AND NOT SHOW THAT SOME MANOEUVER HAS TAKEN PLACE, HOWEVER CLEVERLY IT MAY BE PERFORMED.

NEVERTHELESS UPON OCCASION IT MUST BE EMPLOYED, AND THE RESOURCEFUL PROFESSIONAL FAILING TO IMPROVE THE METHOD CHANGES THE MOMENT; AND BY THIS EXPEDIENT OVERCOMES THE PRINCIPAL OBSTACLE IN THE WAY OF ACCOMPLISHING THE ACTION UNOBSERVED.

THIS SUBTERFUGE IS EXPLAINED IN OUR TREATMENT OF THE SUBJECT, "THE PLAYER WITHOUT AN ALLY," UNDER THE DISTINCTIVE HEADING, "SHIFTING THE CUT."

THE FIRST SHIFT DESCRIBED IS EXECUTED WITH BOTH HANDS AND IS A GREAT FAVORITE.

IT IS PROBABLY THE OLDEST AND BEST IN GENERAL USE.

TWO-HANDED SHIFT

HOLD THE DECK IN THE LEFT HAND, THE THUMB ON ONE SIDE, THE FIRST, SECOND AND THIRD FINGERS CURLED AROUND THE OTHER SIDE WITH THE FIRST JOINTS PRESSING AGAINST THE TOP OF THE DECK AND THE LITTLE FINGER INSERTED AT THE CUT, OR BETWEEN THE TWO PACKETS THAT ARE TO BE REVERSED.

THE DECK IS HELD SLANTINGLY, WITH THE RIGHT SIDE DOWNWARD.

BRING UP THE RIGHT HAND AND COVER THE DECK, SEIZING THE LOWER PACKET BY THE ENDS BETWEEN THE THUMB AND SECOND FINGER, ABOUT HALF AN INCH FROM THE UPPER CORNERS, THE RIGHT-HAND FINGERS BEING CLOSE TOGETHER

BUT NONE OF THEM TOUCHING THE DECK BUT THE THUMB AND SECOND FINGER. (SEE FIG. 49.)

Fig. 49

IF THIS POSITION IS PROPERLY TAKEN THE RIGHT HAND HOLDS THE LOWER PACKET AND THE LEFT HAND CLIPS THE UPPER PACKET BETWEEN THE LITTLE FINGER AND THE OTHER THREE.

NOW, TO REVERSE THE POSITION OF THE TWO PACKETS, THE RIGHT HAND HOLDS THE LOWER PACKET FIRMLY AGAINST THE LEFT THUMB, AND THE LEFT FINGERS DRAW OFF THE UPPER PACKET, UNDER COVER OF THE RIGHT HAND (SEE FIG. 50),

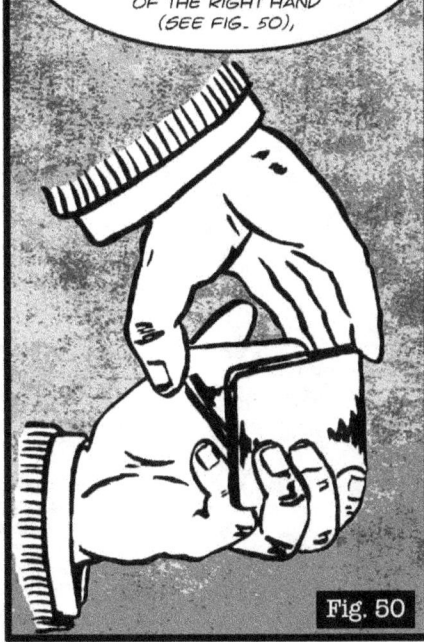

Fig. 50

SO THAT IT JUST CLEARS THE SIDE OF THE LOWER PACKET, AND THEN SWING IT IN UNDERNEATH. (SEE FIG. 51.)

Fig. 51

THE LEFT THUMB AIDS THE TWO PACKETS TO CLEAR EACH OTHER BY PRESSING DOWN ON THE SIDE OF THE UNDER PACKET, SO AS TO TILT UP THE OPPOSITE SIDE AS THE UPPER PACKET IS DRAWN OFF.

THE UNDER PACKET BEING HELD BY ONLY ONE FINGER AND THUMB, CAN BE TILTED AS THOUGH IT WORKED ON A SWIVEL AT EACH END, AND THE RIGHT FINGERS MAY RETAIN THEIR RELATIVE POSITIONS THROUGHOUT.

MOST TEACHERS ADVISE ASSISTING THE ACTION BY HAVING THE FINGERS OF THE RIGHT HAND PULL UP ON THE LOWER PACKET,

BUT WE BELIEVE THE BLIND IS MUCH MORE PERFECT IF THERE IS NOT THE LEAST CHANGE IN THE **ATTITUDE** OF THE RIGHT FINGERS DURING OR IMMEDIATELY AFTER THE SHIFT.

THE PACKETS CAN BE REVERSED LIKE A FLASH, AND WITHOUT THE LEAST NOISE, BUT IT REQUIRES CONSIDERABLE PRACTICE TO ACCOMPLISH THE FEAT PERFECTLY.

THE POSITIONS MUST BE ACCURATELY SECURED AND THE ACTION PERFORMED SLOWLY UNTIL ACCUSTOMED TO THE MOVEMENTS.

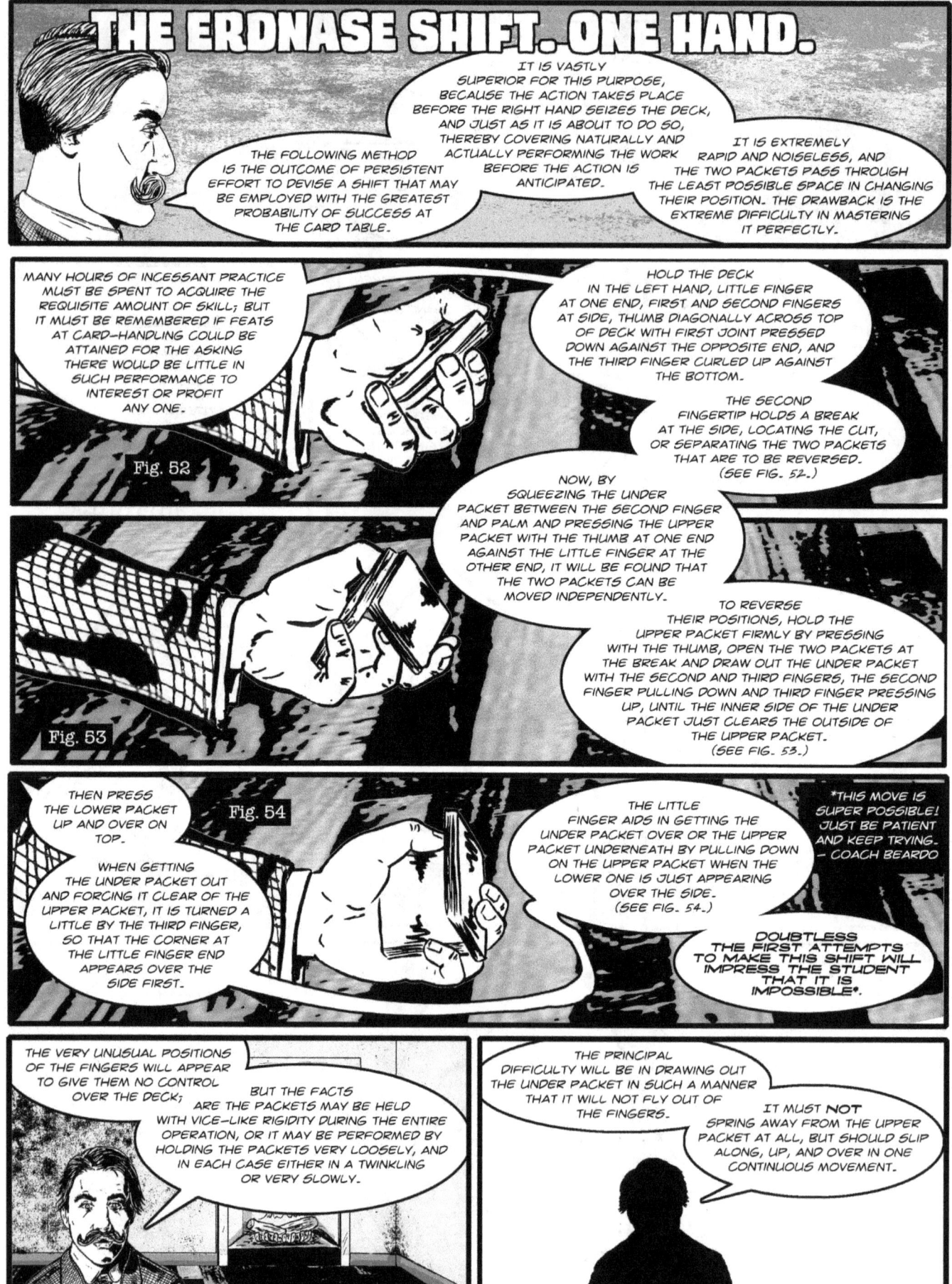

THE GLIMPSE IS OBTAINED BY SLIGHTLY IN-JOGGING THE TOP CARD OF THE LEFT-HAND PACKET, AS EXPLAINED IN TREATMENT OF "BLIND RIFFLES," UNDER CAPTION, "NO. I TO RETAIN TOP STOCK." AS THE THUMBS RAISE THE CORNERS OF THE TWO PACKETS TO RIFFLE, THE TOP CARD IS SLIGHTLY JOGGED OVER AND RAISED BY THE LEFT THUMB, JUST BARELY ENOUGH TO OBTAIN A GLANCE AT THE INDEX, AND WHEN THE CARDS ARE RIFFLED THE CARD SEEN IS LEFT ON TOP, AS IT NATURALLY SHOULD BE. (SEE FIG. 56.)

Fig 56

IT IS QUITE POSSIBLE TO GET A GLIMPSE WITHOUT JOGGING THE CARD IF THE CARDS ARE SPRUNG IN THE USUAL MANNER AND THE LAST ONE RETAINED FOR AN INSTANT IN A SLIGHTLY ELEVATED POSITION BY THE LEFT THUMB.

BUT THIS OPERATION IS MORE LIABLE OF DETECTION. THE OPPORTUNE MOMENT, BOTH TO JOG AND TO GET THE GLIMPSE, IS AFTER THE CORNERS ARE RAISED AND AS THE THUMBS ARE ABOUT TO RELEASE THE CARDS.

THE TOP CARD IS BROUGHT TO THE BOTTOM BY A RUSE WORKED IN CONNECTION WITH THE BLIND CUT, DESCRIBED UNDER HEADING OF "NO. IV. TO RETAIN BOTTOM STOCK."*

*WAY BACK ON PAGE 30!—DT

AN UNDER-CUT IS MADE WITH THE RIGHT HAND, AND AS THE PACKET IS PLACED ON TOP IT IS DONE WITH A SIDLING MOVEMENT, THE TIP OF THE RIGHT THUMB LIGHTLY SLIDES ACROSS THE TOP CARD OF THE THEN UNDER PACKET, PUSHING IT A LITTLE OVER THE INNER SIDE.

THE LEFT THUMB IS AT THE SIDE TO RECEIVE IT, AND FORMS A BREAK, SO THAT IT BECOMES THE UNDER CARD OF THE TOP PACKET WHEN SQUARED UP.

THEN THE BLIND CUT IS EXECUTED AS DESCRIBED, THE TOP PACKET TO THE BREAK IS DRAWN OFF FIRST, AND THE REST OF THE DECK IN SEVERAL PACKETS, AND THE PARTICULAR CARD IS LEFT AT THE BOTTOM.

THE RIFFLE IS AGAIN EXECUTED, RETAINING THIS CARD AT THE BOTTOM, THE GLIMPSE OBTAINED OF THE NEXT TOP CARD OF THE LEFT-HAND PACKET, WHICH IS BROUGHT DOWN IN LIKE MANNER, AND SO ON.

THESE CARDS MIGHT BE LEFT ON TOP, BUT THEY WOULD BE OF LITTLE USE THERE.

IF AT THE BOTTOM, THE KNOWLEDGE OF TWO OR THREE CARDS IS OF IMMENSE **ADVANTAGE** TO AN EXPERT.

WHEN PLAYING ALONE HE EITHER DEALS WITHOUT REPLACING ON THE CUT, OR PALMS FOR THE CUT, OR SHIFTS AFTER THE CUT.

IF HE HAS AN ALLY ON HIS RIGHT A BLIND CUT IS MADE.

IN ANY CASE HE DEALS THE CARDS FROM THE BOTTOM, TO HIMSELF IF THEY ARE DESIRABLE, AND TO AN OPPONENT IF NOT.

MODE OF HOLDING THE HAND

THE PROFESSIONAL PLAYER, EVER CONSCIOUS OF THE NECESSITY OF UNIFORMITY, WILL ALWAYS HOLD HIS HAND IN THE SAME MANNER; AND AS HE OFTEN FINDS IT CONVENIENT TO HAVE MORE THAN HIS SHARE OF THE CARDS, THE POSITION MUST BE ONE WHICH WILL ALWAYS DISGUISE THAT POSSIBILITY. THE BEST FOR ALL PURPOSES IS AS FOLLOWS:

HOLD THE CARDS IN THE LEFT HAND, THE END FITTING INTO THE THIRD JOINTS OF THE FIRST, SECOND AND THIRD FINGERS, THE LOWER CORNER RESTING ON THE LITTLE FINGER CLOSE TO THE THIRD JOINT, AND THE LITTLE FINGER CURLED IN SO THAT THE CARDS REST ON THE FIRST JOINT ALSO.

THE LEFT THUMB RESTS ON THE UPPER SIDE, AND THE FIRST, SECOND AND THIRD FINGERS ARE CURLED IN SO THAT THEIR TIPS REST AGAINST THE BACK.

Fig. 58

THEN, HOLDING THIS CARD FIRMLY, AND KEEPING THE RIGHT HAND ALMOST STATIONARY, PULL OUT THE REST OF THE CARDS WITH THE LEFT HAND BY A BACKWARD AND INWARD MOTION AND BY PRESSING THE LEFT FINGERTIPS AGAINST THE BACK. (SEE FIG. 58.)

THEN SHOVE THE RIGHT-HAND CARD ON TOP.

THE ACTION IS NOT CONCEALED, BUT MADE OPENLY.

IT IS A VERY COMMON PROCEDURE FOR ARRANGING ANY HAND FOR PLAY OR DISCARD.

IF THE DISCARD HAPPEN TO LIE TOGETHER, BRING THEM TO THE TOP WITH ONE ACTION.

NOW THE TOP CARDS MUST BE PALMED, AND ONE OF THE METHODS ALREADY DESCRIBED IN THIS WORK MAY BE EMPLOYED.

BUT FOR USE IN THIS PARTICULAR CASE WE WOULD ADVISE ANOTHER PALM, WHICH IS MOST FITTING FOR A DISCARD, AND ESPECIALLY THE MOVEMENTS LEADING UP TO THE ACTUAL PALMING.

FORM A BREAK BETWEEN THE DISCARD AND THE REST AND HOLD THE BREAK WITH THE RIGHT THUMB.

SHIFT THE LEFT THUMB TO THE OUTER-END CORNER OF THE UNDER PACKET, AND SLIDE IT DOWN ABOUT HALF AN INCH INTO THE RIGHT PALM.

CLOSE THE BREAK, HOLD CARDS WITH LEFT HAND, RELEASE THE RIGHT AND PUSH THE CARDS FURTHER DOWN INTO THE RIGHT PALM BETWEEN BASE OF THUMB AND THIRD AND LITTLE FINGERS,

SUFFICIENTLY TO ALLOW TIPS OF RIGHT THUMB AND SECOND FINGER TO REACH THE OUTER-END CORNERS OVER THE LEFT THUMB AND LITTLE FINGER. (SEE FIG. 59.)

Fig. 59

NOW RELEASE THE LEFT HAND ENTIRELY AND TURN THE RIGHT PALM DOWNWARD.

THIS POSITION COVERS THE SIDES AND THE INNER END COMPLETELY, CONCEALING THE QUANTITY, AND THE FACT THAT THE PACKETS OVERLAP, AND YET HAS A VERY EASY AND NATURAL APPEARANCE. (SEE FIG. 60.)

Fig. 60

THE RIGHT HAND CAN NOW NONCHALANTLY HOLD THE CARDS, WHILE THE LEFT HANDLES THE CHIPS OR MAKES A BET.

WHEN READY TO DEAL AGAIN, THE LEFT HAND SEIZES THE CARDS FROM BELOW, AT THE MIDDLE OF SIDES, BETWEEN SECOND AND THIRD FINGERS AND THUMB, AND THE LITTLE FINGER ON THE PROTRUDING CORNER OF THE UNDER PACKET, AND AT THE SAME MOMENT THE RIGHT FOUR FINGERS ARE SHIFTED TO THE OUTER END AS IF TO TAKE THE FRESH HOLD.

PRESS DOWN ON THE OUTER END, HOLD INNER PROTRUDING END WITH LEFT LITTLE FINGER, RELEASE THE UPPER PACKET WHICH IS HELD BY THE LEFT THUMB AND SECOND AND THIRD FINGERS (SEE FIG. 61), AND IT WILL SPRING UP INTO THE RIGHT PALM.

Fig. 61

THE LEFT HAND INSTANTLY DRAWS THE UNDER PACKET OUT SIDEWAYS ABOUT HALF WAY, AND THE RIGHT HAND DROPS IT ON THE TABLE AND THEN PLACES THE PALMED CARDS ON THE DECK **WHILE** PICKING IT UP.

THIS METHOD OF PALMING IS EXCELLENT AFTER THE POSITION IS SECURED, AND UNDER THE CIRCUMSTANCES JUST DESCRIBED IT IS BETTER TO TAKE THIS POSITION THAN TO MAKE THE PALM IMMEDIATELY AFTER THE HAND IS SKINNED.

IF IT IS DESIRED TO PALM IN THE LEFT HAND, THE DISCARD IS RETAINED AND THE OTHERS BROUGHT TO THE TOP WHILE SKINNING.

THEN ONE OF THE BOTTOM PALMS DESCRIBED MUST BE EMPLOYED.

THE PLAYER WITHOUT AN ALLY.

IT IS THE GENERAL BELIEF THAT IT TAKES TWO TO OBTAIN ANY ADVANTAGE IN A CARD GAME WITH KNOWING PLAYERS—THE DEALER AND THE MAN WHO CUTS.

THAT THIS IS GENERALLY TRUE CANNOT BE DENIED, BUT IT IS BY NO MEANS ALWAYS SO.

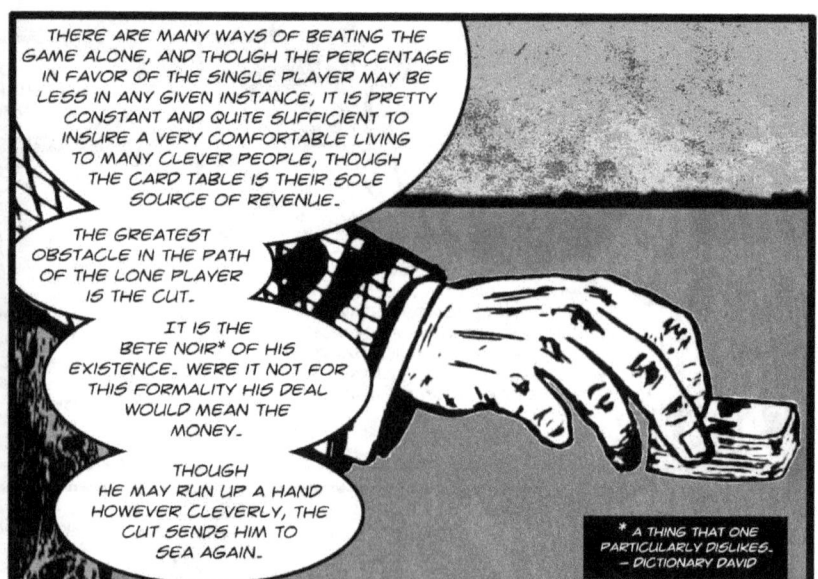

THERE ARE MANY WAYS OF BEATING THE GAME ALONE, AND THOUGH THE PERCENTAGE IN FAVOR OF THE SINGLE PLAYER MAY BE LESS IN ANY GIVEN INSTANCE, IT IS PRETTY CONSTANT AND QUITE SUFFICIENT TO INSURE A VERY COMFORTABLE LIVING TO MANY CLEVER PEOPLE, THOUGH THE CARD TABLE IS THEIR SOLE SOURCE OF REVENUE.

THE GREATEST OBSTACLE IN THE PATH OF THE LONE PLAYER IS THE CUT.

IT IS THE BETE NOIR* OF HIS EXISTENCE. WERE IT NOT FOR THIS FORMALITY HIS DEAL WOULD MEAN THE MONEY.

THOUGH HE MAY RUN UP A HAND HOWEVER CLEVERLY, THE CUT SENDS HIM TO SEA AGAIN.

* A THING THAT ONE PARTICULARLY DISLIKES. — DICTIONARY DAVID

"PUT YOUR FAITH IN PROVIDENCE, BUT ALWAYS CUT THE CARDS,"* IS A WISE INJUNCTION.

SOMETIMES THE CUT IS NOT MADE, AND THE ADEPT DEARLY LOVES TO SIT ON THE LEFT OF A PLAYER WHO IS CARELESS ENOUGH TO OCCASIONALLY SAY, "RUN THEM"—I. E., HE WAIVES THE CUT.

PROFESSIONAL PLAYERS ALWAYS CALCULATE ON SUCH A POSSIBILITY, AND WILL CONTINUE TO STOCK ON EVERY DEAL TO SOME EXTENT WITH THAT CHANCE IN VIEW.

DEALING WITHOUT THE CUT.

WHEN THE DEALER HAS DESIRED CARDS ON THE BOTTOM AND THE CUT IS MADE WITHOUT REPLACING THE TWO PACKETS, HE WILL PICK UP THE PACKET THAT WAS UNDER AND IMMEDIATELY PROCEED TO DEAL FROM THAT ALONE.

IN THIS WAY HE CAN GET THE UNDER CARDS BY BOTTOM DEALING.

FIG. 25 FROM PAGE 36 – DT

THE CUT IS USUALLY MADE IN THIS WAY, AND THE DEALER AIDS THE PLAY BY BEING READY TO SEIZE THE UNDER PACKET AS THE TOP IS LIFTED OFF.

HOWEVER, IF THE COMPANY WILL NOT STAND FOR THIS, AND SOME ONE SAYS, "CARRY THE CUT," HE WILL, OF COURSE, DO SO IN FUTURE AND TURN HIS ATTENTION TO OTHER MANOEUVERS.

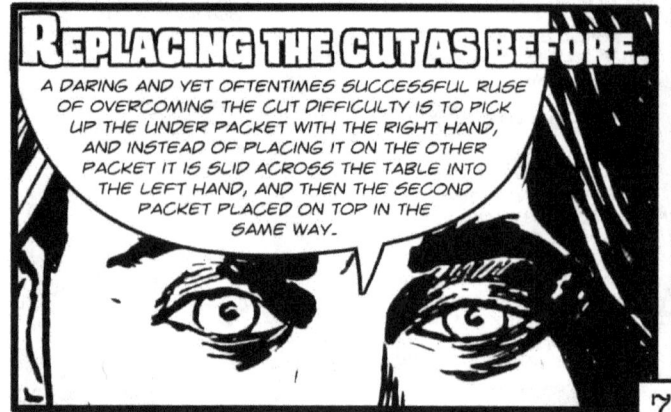

REPLACING THE CUT AS BEFORE.

A DARING AND YET OFTENTIMES SUCCESSFUL RUSE OF OVERCOMING THE CUT DIFFICULTY IS TO PICK UP THE UNDER PACKET WITH THE RIGHT HAND, AND INSTEAD OF PLACING IT ON THE OTHER PACKET IT IS SLID ACROSS THE TABLE INTO THE LEFT HAND, AND THEN THE SECOND PACKET PLACED ON TOP IN THE SAME WAY.

THE PACKETS MAY BE PICKED UP BY THE RIGHT HAND INSTEAD OF SLIDING THEM.

THE MOVE IS MADE QUITE OPENLY, CARELESSLY AND WITHOUT HASTE, AND IS SURPRISINGLY REGULAR IN APPEARANCE. IT WILL NOT PASS IN FAST COMPANY, BUT THE BEAUTY OF IT IS THAT IF NOTICED IT CAN BE ATTRIBUTED TO THOUGHTLESSNESS.

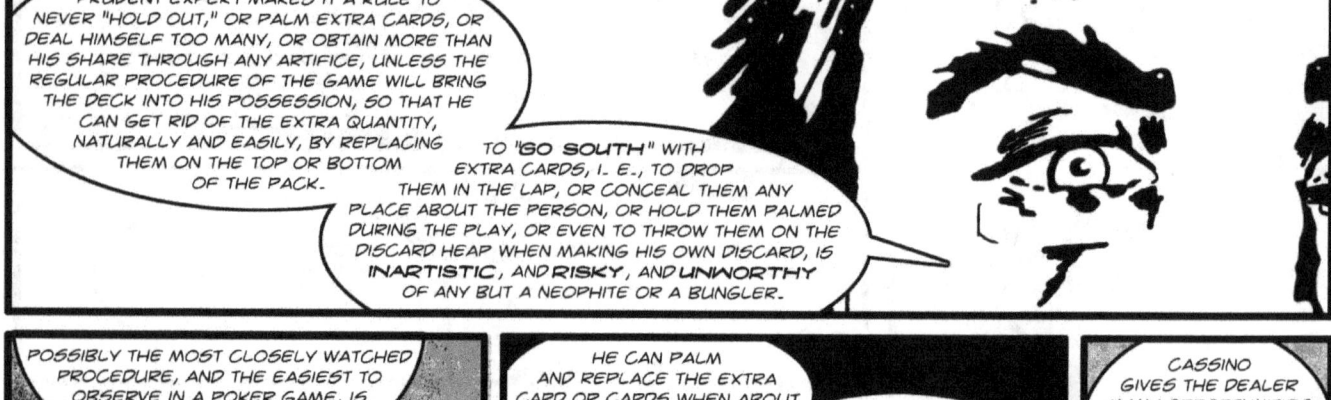

THE CAUTIOUS AND PRUDENT EXPERT MAKES IT A RULE TO NEVER "HOLD OUT," OR PALM EXTRA CARDS, OR DEAL HIMSELF TOO MANY, OR OBTAIN MORE THAN HIS SHARE THROUGH ANY ARTIFICE, UNLESS THE REGULAR PROCEDURE OF THE GAME WILL BRING THE DECK INTO HIS POSSESSION, SO THAT HE CAN GET RID OF THE EXTRA QUANTITY, NATURALLY AND EASILY, BY REPLACING THEM ON THE TOP OR BOTTOM OF THE PACK.

TO "GO SOUTH" WITH EXTRA CARDS, I. E., TO DROP THEM IN THE LAP, OR CONCEAL THEM ANY PLACE ABOUT THE PERSON, OR HOLD THEM PALMED DURING THE PLAY, OR EVEN TO THROW THEM ON THE DISCARD HEAP WHEN MAKING HIS OWN DISCARD, IS **INARTISTIC**, AND **RISKY**, AND **UNWORTHY** OF ANY BUT A NEOPHITE OR A BUNGLER.

POSSIBLY THE MOST CLOSELY WATCHED PROCEDURE, AND THE EASIEST TO OBSERVE IN A POKER GAME, IS THE NUMBER OF CARDS THAT ARE DISCARDED:

AND WHERE THERE IS THE LEAST SUSPICION, DISCARDING TOO MANY IN THE ORDINARY WAY IS SURELY DETECTED. WHEN PLAYING POKER THE EXPERT WILL HOLD TOO MANY ONLY ON HIS OWN DEAL, AND THEN ONLY BEFORE THE DRAW.

HE CAN PALM AND REPLACE THE EXTRA CARD OR CARDS WHEN ABOUT TO DEAL THE DRAW.

IN CRIBBAGE THE NON-DEALER MAY HOLD OUT ONE OR TWO CARDS, AND AFTER THE CRIB IS LAID OUT, REPLACE THE EXTRA CARD WHEN CUTTING FOR THE TURN-UP.

BUT IN WHATSOEVER GAME, WHERE CARDS ARE HELD OUT AT ALL, THE RULE HOLDS GOOD THAT THEY MUST BE RESTORED, AND AT A MOMENT WHEN THE REGULAR PROCEDURE OF THE GAME NECESSITATES THE HANDLING OF THE DECK.

CASSINO GIVES THE DEALER MANY OPPORTUNITIES OF HOLDING TOO MANY, AS THE DECK IS CONTINUOUSLY HANDLED DURING THE GAME.

THE SHORT DECK

A SIMPLE METHOD OF OBTAINING AN ADVANTAGE IN MANY GAMES IS THAT OF PLAYING WITH A "SHORT" DECK.

SEVERAL CARDS ARE REMOVED ENTIRELY FROM THE PACK, BUT RETAINED IN THE MEMORY, AND THE GAME IS PLAYED WITHOUT THEM.

THE KNOWLEDGE THAT THESE PARTICULAR CARDS ARE WITHHELD ENABLES THE STRATEGIST TO MAKE HIS CALCULATIONS AND PLAY HIS OWN CARDS WITH A GREAT DEAL MORE CERTAINTY.

CARDS HELD OUT ENTIRELY ARE USUALLY DESTROYED, OR OTHERWISE EFFECTUALLY DISPOSED OF, SO AS TO PRECLUDE THE POSSIBILITY OF THE SCHEMER BEING DISCOVERED "WITH THE GOODS ON HIM."

A VERY BOLD EXPEDIENT AT TWO-HANDED CASSINO IS TO DISPOSE OF EIGHT CARDS.

THIS RUNS THE DECK TO FIVE DEALS INSTEAD OF SIX.

THE LOWER CARDS ARE USUALLY SELECTED, AND OF DIFFERENT DENOMINATIONS, SAY THE FOUR AND SIX OF SPADES, AND THE DEUCE, TRAY, FOUR, FIVE, SEVEN AND EIGHT OF OTHER SUITS.

WITH THIS ARRANGEMENT, OR DEPLETION, AN ADVERSARY ENJOYING ORDINARY LUCK, WILL FIND IN SUMMING UP HIS POINTS THAT HE DOES NOT MAKE "CARDS" OR "SPADES" IN A VERY LONG TIME INDEED, AND OF COURSE HE CREDITS HIS OPPONENT WITH THREE POINTS.

THE IDEA OF SO MANY CARDS BEING WITHHELD FROM THE DECK WITHOUT BEING NOTICED, WILL DOUBTLESS CAUSE CERTAIN CASSINO PLAYERS TO SMILE.

WE DON'T THINK MANY SHREWD PLAYERS COULD BE SO IMPOSED UPON, BUT WE REGRET THE TRUTH OF THE CONFESSION THAT ONCE UPON A TIME WE WERE, AND WE MARVELED GREATLY AND ALSO SORROWED, OVER A CONTINUOUS AND VERY PROTRACTED RUN OF "HARD LUCK."

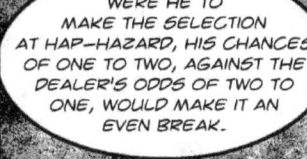

THE PROPER WAY TO INTRODUCE IT IS TO MAKE THE THROW SEVERAL TIMES IN THE NATURAL ORDER, THAT IS, BY DROPPING THE UNDER CARD FIRST, WHILE EXPLAINING THE GAME TO THE COMPANY.

THE ACE SHOULD BE PICKED UP BY EITHER HAND IN THE ORDER IT HAPPENS TO FALL, AND BE HELD AT EITHER THE TOP OR BOTTOM POSITION IN THE RIGHT HAND, AND THE FACES SHOWN BEFORE EACH THROW.

THEN THE BLIND THROW IS MADE AND THE GUESSING AND FUN BEGINS.

WHEN THE DEAL IS PERFORMED BY A FINISHED ARTIST, IT IS ABSOLUTELY IMPOSSIBLE FOR THE KEENEST EYE TO DETECT THE RUSE.

EVEN WHEN THE PROCESS, OR NATURE OF THE BLIND IS UNDERSTOOD, THE PLAYER HAS NO GREATER ADVANTAGE SAVE THAT HE KNOWS ENOUGH NOT TO BET.

THE PARTICULAR CARD CANNOT BE FOLLOWED WITH THE EYE, AND IF THE KNOWING PLAYER WERE TO BET ON A BLIND THROW ONCE, THE DEALER CAN MAKE HIS NEXT THROW REGULAR.

THE DEALER HIMSELF IS AS HOPELESSLY LOST, IF GUESSING AGAINST ANOTHER WHO CAN THROW EQUALLY AS WELL.

A SECOND METHOD OF MAKING THE THROW OR DEAL IS TO HOLD THE TWO RIGHT-HAND CARDS BETWEEN THE SECOND FINGER AND THUMB ONLY, THE RIGHT THIRD FINGER TAKING NO PART IN THE ACTION AND BEING HELD RATHER OSTENTATIOUSLY STRAIGHT OUT.

WHEN THE TOP CARD IS THROWN, THE LEFT LITTLE FINGER IS MOVED IN UNDER THE END OF THE THIRD FINGER, AND THE TIP CATCHES AND HOLDS THE CORNER OF THE LOWER CARD, WHILE THE SECOND FINGER RELEASES BOTH, SO AS TO LET THE TOP CARD FALL.

THEN THE SECOND FINGER INSTANTLY RETAKES ITS ORIGINAL POSITION, AND THE LITTLE FINGER IS RELEASED. THE ACTION OF THE LITTLE FINGER IS COMPLETELY COVERED BY THE POSITION OF THE THIRD FINGER.

THIS METHOD IS PERHAPS MORE SUBTLE, AS IT APPEARS QUITE IMPOSSIBLE TO THROW THE TOP CARD WITHOUT DROPPING BOTH.

AN ADDITION TO THE GAME IS MADE BY PUTTING IN A CRIMP OR UPTURN IN A CORNER OF THE ACE.

THEN SEVERAL THROWS ARE MADE, AND A PLAYER FINDS HE CAN LOCATE THE ACE "JUST FOR FUN" EVERY TIME.

WHEN PERFECT CONFIDENCE IS INSPIRED, AND THE CUPIDITY OF THE PLAYER TEMPTS HIM TO COVER THE ODDS, A THROW IS MADE, THE PLAYER SELECTS THE CARD WITH THE CORNER TURNED, AND IS AMAZED TO FIND HE HAS MISSED THE "CINCH."

IN A CONFIDENCE GAME, THE CORNER OF THE ACE IS TURNED BY A "CAPPER," WHO SEIZES AN OPPORTUNITY WHEN THE CARELESS (?) DEALER TURNS TO EXPECTORATE, OR ON ANY PRETEXT NEGLECTS HIS GAME FOR A MOMENT.

BUT THE CRIMP CAN BE PUT IN, TAKEN OUT, AND AGAIN PUT IN THE CORNER OF ANOTHER CARD DURING THE PROCEDURE OF THE THROW.

TO CRIMP THE CORNER, PICK UP THE ACE WITH THE SECOND FINGER AND THUMB OF RIGHT HAND, SECOND FINGER AT MIDDLE OF END, AND LET THE THIRD FINGERTIP REST ON TOP OF THE CARD CLOSE TO SECOND FINGER.

THEN CATCH THE CORNER WITH THE LITTLE FINGER AND SQUEEZE IT IN, PRESSING DOWN WITH THIRD FINGERTIP, AND THE CORNER IS CRIMPED UPWARD.

THE CORNER IS TURNED DOWN AGAIN BY SLIPPING THE THIRD FINGER TIP OVER THE END, AND PULLING UP; AND PRESSING DOWN ON THE CORNER WITH THE LITTLE FINGERTIP.

EITHER ACTION CAN BE PERFORMED IN AN INSTANT AS THE CARD IS PICKED UP.

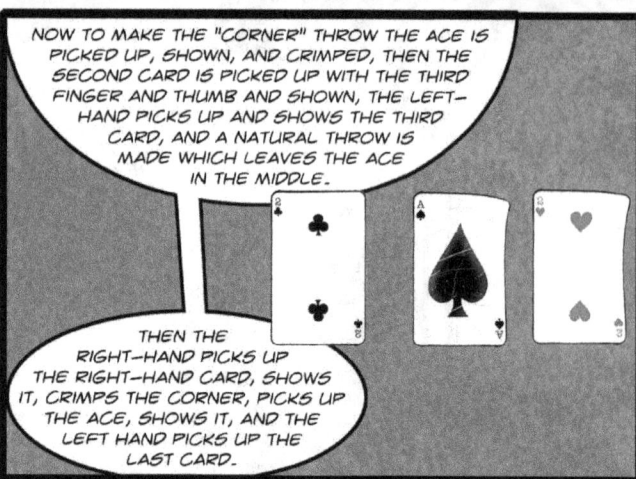
NOW TO MAKE THE "CORNER" THROW THE ACE IS PICKED UP, SHOWN, AND CRIMPED, THEN THE SECOND CARD IS PICKED UP WITH THE THIRD FINGER AND THUMB AND SHOWN, THE LEFT-HAND PICKS UP AND SHOWS THE THIRD CARD, AND A NATURAL THROW IS MADE WHICH LEAVES THE ACE IN THE MIDDLE.

THEN THE RIGHT-HAND PICKS UP THE RIGHT-HAND CARD, SHOWS IT, CRIMPS THE CORNER, PICKS UP THE ACE, SHOWS IT, AND THE LEFT HAND PICKS UP THE LAST CARD.

NOW THE RIGHT HAND HOLDS THE TWO TURNED CORNER CARDS, BUT THE FACT THAT THE UPPER ONE IS CRIMPED CANNOT BE SEEN BECAUSE OF THE POSITIONS OF THE FINGERS, EVEN WHEN THE FACE OF THE UNDER ONE, WHICH IS THE ACE, IS SHOWN.

THIS TIME A BLIND THROW IS MADE, THE RIGHT-HAND DROPPING THE TOP CARD FIRST WITH ITS CORNER TURNED, THEN THE LEFT HAND CARD IS THROWN, AND LONG ERE THIS THE RIGHT-HAND HAS TURNED DOWN THE CORNER OF THE ACE AND IT IS DROPPED INNOCENTLY IN THE MIDDLE.

THE PROCESS OF TURNING AND REVERSING THE CORNERS REQUIRES AS MUCH SKILL AND CLEVERNESS AS MAKING THE THROW.

ALL DETAILS OF THE GAME SHOULD BE PERFECTED BEFORE IT IS ATTEMPTED IN COMPANY, AND NOTHING BUT CAREFUL PRACTICE BEFORE A MIRROR WILL ENABLE AN AMATEUR TO PERFORM THE ACTION IN ANYTHING LIKE A SATISFACTORY MANNER.

BUT THERE IS NOT A SINGLE CARD FEAT IN THE WHOLE CALENDAR THAT WILL GIVE AS GOOD RETURNS FOR THE AMOUNT OF PRACTICE REQUIRED, OR THAT WILL MYSTIFY AS GREATLY, OR CAUSE AS MUCH AMUSEMENT, OR BEAR SO MUCH REPETITION, AS THIS LITTLE GAME;

AND FOR THESE REASONS WE BELIEVE IT WORTHY OF UNSTINTED EFFORT TO MASTER THOROUGHLY.

MEXICAN THREE CARD MONTE.

WHEN THE GAME IS PLAYED IN THE FOLLOWING MANNER THE BETTER HAS NO POSSIBLE CHANCE TO WIN, AND YET IT APPEARS SIMPLER AND EASIER THAN THE OTHER.

AN ENTIRELY DIFFERENT SUBTERFUGE IS EMPLOYED BY THE DEALER.

THE THREE CARDS ARE LEFT PERFECTLY FLAT. SOMETIMES THE FOUR CORNERS ARE TURNED THE VERY LEAST UPWARDS, MERELY ENOUGH TO ALLOW ONE CARD TO BE SLIPPED UNDER THE OTHER WHEN LYING FACE DOWN ON THE TABLE, BUT THE BEND IS NOT NECESSARY.

THE DEALER NOW SHOWS THE FACES OF THE THREE CARDS, AND SLOWLY LAYS THEM IN A ROW.

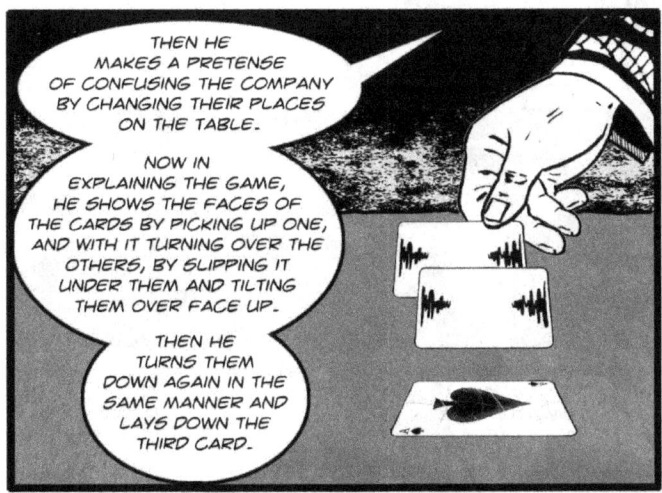

LEGERDEMAIN
PART SECOND

LEGERDEMAIN — SKILLFUL USE OF ONE'S HANDS WHEN PERFORMING CONJURING TRICKS

THERE IS NO BRANCH OF CONJURING THAT SO FULLY REPAYS THE AMATEUR FOR HIS LABOR AND STUDY AS SLIGHT-OF-HAND WITH CARDS.

THE ARTIST IS ALWAYS SURE OF A COMPREHENSIVE AND APPRECIATIVE AUDIENCE.

THERE IS NO AMUSEMENT OR PASTIME IN THE CIVILIZED WORLD SO PREVALENT AS CARD GAMES, AND ALMOST EVERYBODY LOVES A GOOD TRICK.

BUT THE SPECIAL ADVANTAGE IN THIS RESPECT IS THAT THE REALLY CLEVER CARD-HANDLER CAN DISPENSE WITH THE ENDLESS DEVICES AND PREPARATIONS THAT ENCUMBER THE PERFORMER IN OTHER BRANCHES.

HE IS EVER PREPARED FOR THE MOST UNEXPECTED DEMANDS UPON HIS ABILITY TO AMUSE OR MYSTIFY, AND HE CAN SUSTAIN HIS REPUTATION WITH NOTHING BUT THE FAMILY DECK AND HIS NIMBLE FINGERS, MAKING HIS EXHIBITION ALL THE MORE STARTLING BECAUSE OF ITS KNOWN IMPROMPTU NATURE AND SIMPLE ACCESSORIES.

TO THE STUDENT WHO WISHES TO MAKE THE MOST RAPID PROGRESS TOWARD THE ACTUAL PERFORMANCE OF TRICKS, WE SUGGEST THAT HE FIRST TAKE UP THE STUDY AND PRACTICE OF OUR "SYSTEM OF BLIND SHUFFLES" AS TAUGHT IN THE FIRST PART OF THIS BOOK, ACQUIRING THOROUGH PROFICIENCY IN FORMING AND USING THE "JOG" AND "BREAK," WHICH MAKE THIS STYLE OF SHUFFLE POSSIBLE.

WE ARE AWARE THAT ALL CONJURERS ADVISE THE SHIFT OR PASS, AS THE FIRST ACCOMPLISHMENT, AND WHILE WE DO NOT BELITTLE THE MERITS OF THE SHIFT WHEN PERFECTLY PERFORMED, WE INSIST THAT ALL OR ANY OF THE VARIOUS METHODS OF EXECUTING IT, ARE AMONG THE MOST DIFFICULT FEATS THE STUDENT WILL BE CALLED UPON TO ACQUIRE, AND IMPOSING SUCH A TASK AT THE OUTSET HAS A MOST DISCOURAGING EFFECT.

BUT SO FAR AS WE CAN LEARN FROM THE EXHIBITIONS AND LITERATURE OF CONJURERS, NOT ONE OF THEM KNOWS OF, OR AT LEAST EMPLOYS OR WRITES OF, A SATISFACTORY SUBSTITUTE; HENCE THEIR ENTIRE DEPENDENCE UPON THAT ARTIFICE TO PRODUCE CERTAIN RESULTS.

WHEN THE BLIND SHUFFLES WITH THE COINCIDENT JOG AND BREAK, ARE THOROUGHLY UNDERSTOOD, THE STUDENT SHOULD TAKE UP OUR "SYSTEM OF PALMING," ALSO TREATED IN THE FIRST PART, PAYING PARTICULAR ATTENTION TO THE "BOTTOM PALM," AND WITH EVEN A MODERATE DEGREE OF SKILL IN THESE ACCOMPLISHMENTS HE WILL BE ENABLED TO PERFORM MANY OF THE BEST TRICKS THAT CONJURERS MAKE ENTIRELY DEPENDENT ON THE SHIFT.

IN THIS PHASE OF CARD-HANDLING, AS WITH CARD-TABLE ARTIFICE, WE ARE OF THE OPINION THAT THE LESS THE COMPANY KNOWS ABOUT THE DEXTERITY OF THE PERFORMER, THE BETTER IT ANSWERS HIS PURPOSE.

A MUCH GREATER INTEREST IS TAKEN IN THE TRICKS, AND THE DENOUEMENT OF EACH CAUSES INFINITELY MORE AMAZEMENT, WHEN THE ENTIRE PROCEDURE HAS BEEN CONDUCTED IN AN ORDINARY MANNER, AND QUITE FREE OF OSTENSIBLE CLEVERNESS AT PRESTIDIGITATION.

IF THE PERFORMER CANNOT RESIST THE TEMPTATION TO PARADE HIS DIGITAL ABILITY, IT WILL MAR THE EFFECT OF HIS ENDEAVORS MUCH LESS BY ADJURING THE EXHIBITION OF SUCH SLIGHTS AS PALMING AND PRODUCING, SINGLE-HAND SHIFTS, CHANGES, ETC., UNTIL THE WIND UP OF THE ENTERTAINMENT.

BUT THE SLIGHTS SHOULD BE EMPLOYED ONLY AS A MEANS TO AN END.

THE AMATEUR CONJURER WHO IS NOT NATURALLY BLESSED WITH A "GIFT OF THE GAB" SHOULD REHEARSE HIS "PATTER" OR MONOLOGUE AS CAREFULLY AS HIS ACTION.

THE SIMPLEST TRICK SHOULD BE APPROPRIATELY CLOTHED WITH CHICANERY OR PLAUSIBLE SOPHISTRY WHICH APPARENTLY EXPLAINS THE PROCEDURE, BUT IN REALITY DESCRIBES ABOUT THE CONTRARY OF WHAT TAKES PLACE.

THE PRINCIPAL SLIGHTS EMPLOYED IN CARD TRICKS, THAT ARE NOT TOUCHED UPON IN THE FIRST PART OF THIS BOOK, ARE KNOWN AS "FORCING," "CHANGES," "TRANSFORMATIONS," AND VARIOUS METHODS OF LOCATING AND PRODUCING SELECTED CARDS.

WE SHALL ALSO DESCRIBE OTHER METHODS OF SHIFTING AND PALMING.

WE SHOULD MENTION THAT A SHIFT IS TERMED BY THE CONJURER A "PASS."

SHIFTS
SINGLE-HANDED SHIFT.

THIS IS KNOWN TO CONJURERS AS THE "CHARLIER PASS," AND WE PRESUME WAS INVENTED BY THE FAMOUS MAGICIAN OF THAT NAME.

HOLD THE DECK IN THE LEFT HAND FACE DOWN, BETWEEN THE THUMB TIP AT ONE SIDE AND FIRST JOINTS OF SECOND AND THIRD FINGERS AT OPPOSITE SIDE, FIRST JOINT OF LITTLE FINGER AT END, AND FIRST FINGER EXTENDED AT BOTTOM.

TO MAKE THE SHIFT RELEASE THE LOWER PORTION OF THE DECK WITH THE THUMB, LETTING IT FALL INTO THE PALM (SEE FIG. 65),

THEN PUSH UP THE FINGER SIDE OF THE FALLEN PORTION, WITH THE FIRST FINGER TIP, UNTIL IT REACHES THE THUMB WHICH IS STILL SUPPORTING THE UPPER PORTION.

NOW EXTEND THE SECOND AND THIRD FINGERS SLIGHTLY SO THAT THE THUMB SIDE OF THE UPPER PORTION WILL PASS THE UPTURNED SIDE OF THE LOWER PORTION (SEE FIG. 66),

THEN STRAIGHTEN OUT THE FIRST FINGER ALLOWING THE UPPER PORTION TO DROP DOWN INTO THE PALM AND THE LOWER PORTION ON TOP OF IT.

THE LITTLE FINGER HELD AT THE MIDDLE OF THE END IS OF GREAT ASSISTANCE IN THIS SHIFT, GIVING BETTER CONTROL OF BOTH PORTIONS, AND ENABLING THE PERFORMER TO HOLD THE DECK MUCH NEARER A VERTICAL POSITION.

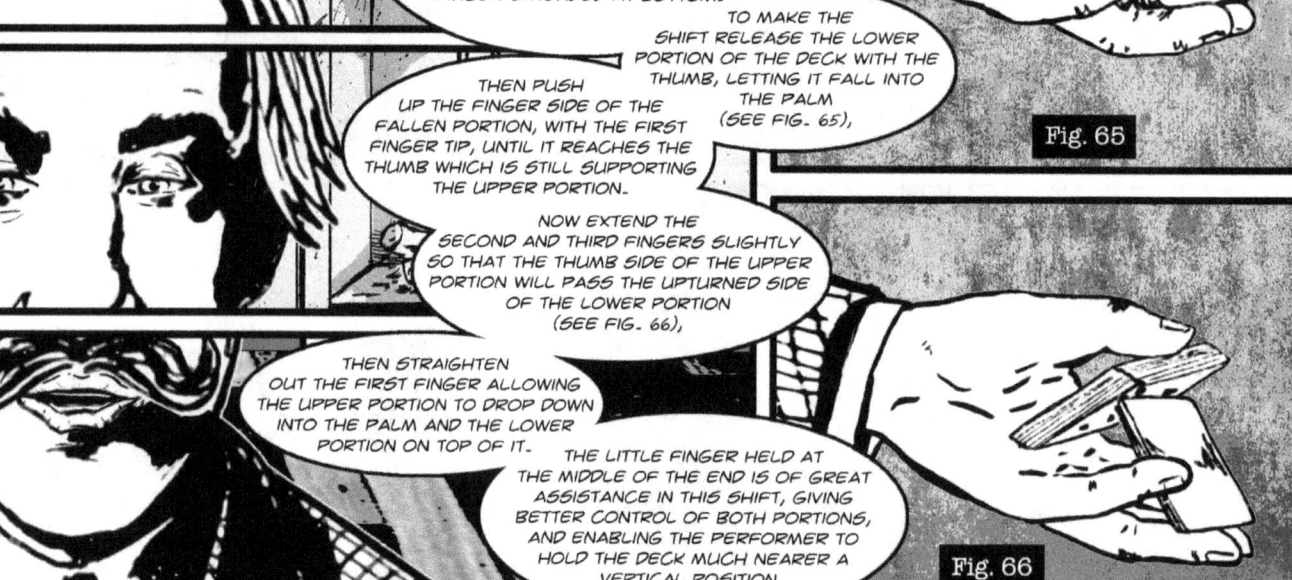

Fig. 65

Fig. 66

THE LONGITUDINAL SHIFT.

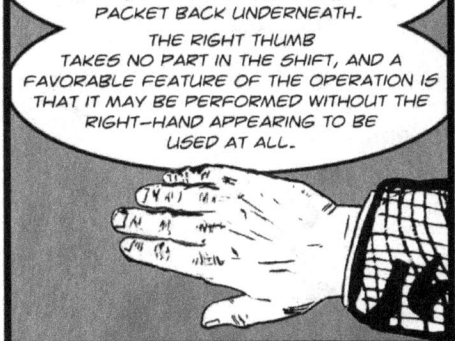

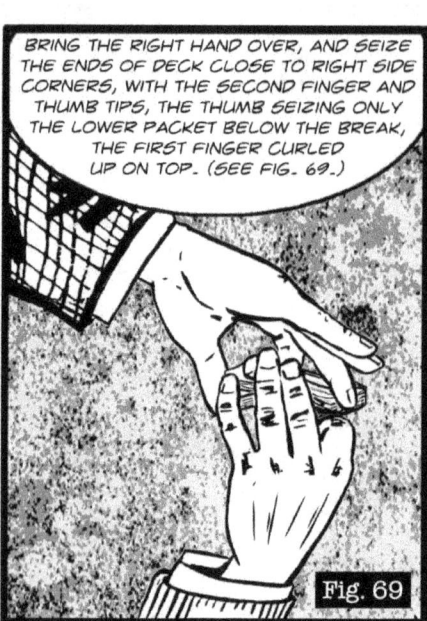

THE S.W.E. SHIFT

WE HAVE NOT DUBBED THE FOLLOWING PROCESS WITH OUR INITIALS BECAUSE WE WISH TO APPEAR "BIG ON THE BILLS," BUT MERELY TO GIVE IT A NAME.

STILL, WE MUST CONFESS TO SOME SATISFACTION IN HAVING ORIGINATED WHAT WE BELIEVE TO BE THE MOST RAPID, AND, FOR CERTAIN PURPOSES, THE MOST PERFECT SHIFT EVER DEVISED.

THE METHOD IS PRACTICALLY THE SAME AS THE "LONGITUDINAL," BUT AS THE DECK IS HELD CROSSWISE IT IS MUCH MORE RAPID. THE POSITION IS OPEN AND NATURAL, AND THE SHIFT POSSESSES MANY ADVANTAGES FOR CONJURING PURPOSES.

HOLD THE DECK IN THE LEFT HAND, FACE DOWN, FIRST JOINT OF THE THUMB AGAINST MIDDLE OF ONE END, SECOND, THIRD AND LITTLE FINGERS AGAINST THE OPPOSITE OR LOWER END, LITTLE FINGER HOLDING A BREAK BETWEEN THE TWO PACKETS AT END, BY THE CORNER OF THE LOWER PACKET BEING BETWEEN THE LITTLE AND THIRD FINGERS, THE LITTLE FINGER LYING PARTIALLY ACROSS THE CORNER OF THE UNDER PACKET. (SEE FIG. 71.)

THIS POSITION, LIKE THAT OF THE "LONGITUDINAL," ALLOWS THE TIPS OF THE SECOND, THIRD AND LITTLE FINGERS TO APPEAR OVER THE TOP OF THE DECK, AND THE FACT THAT THERE IS A BREAK IS NOT APPARENT TO A SPECTATOR. THE FIRST FINGER IS CURLED UP AGAINST THE BOTTOM.

Fig. 71

Fig. 71.b

THE BREAK IS HELD ONLY AT THE LOWER END, AND AT THE INSIDE, THE OTHER FINGERS AND THUMB HOLDING THE PACKET FIRMLY TOGETHER.

NOW BRING THE RIGHT HAND OVER THE LOWER OR RIGHT-HAND END OF THE DECK, AND SEIZE THE SIDES CLOSE AS POSSIBLE TO THE LOWER CORNERS, BETWEEN THE SECOND AND THIRD FINGER-TIPS AND THUMB, THE FIRST FINGER CURLED UP ON TOP OUT OF THE WAY.

THIS LEAVES AT LEAST TWO-THIRDS OF THE DECK IN VIEW. (SEE FIG. 72.)

Fig. 72

Fig. 72.b

TO MAKE THE SHIFT RAISE THE RIGHT THUMB TO THE EDGE OF THE SIDE, DRAW THE TOP PACKET IN AND DOWN WITH THE LEFT THUMB AND LITTLE FINGER, AND PRESS THE LOWER PACKET OUT AND DOWN, BETWEEN THE RIGHT SECOND AND THIRD FINGER TIPS AND THE LEFT FIRST FINGER WHICH IS CURLED UP UNDERNEATH; THE LEFT SECOND FINGER AT THE END HELPS TO CONTROL THE LOWER PACKET AS IT IS PRESSED OUT.

THIS ACTION WILL TILT THE OPPOSITE SIDES OF BOTH PACKETS UPWARDS, AND AS THEY CLEAR EACH OTHER THE RIGHT THUMB TIP CATCHES THE UNDER PACKET, AND THE LEFT THIRD FINGER CATCHES THE UPPER PACKET AND IT IS BROUGHT BACK UNDERNEATH. (SEE FIG. 73.)

Fig. 73

Fig. 73.b

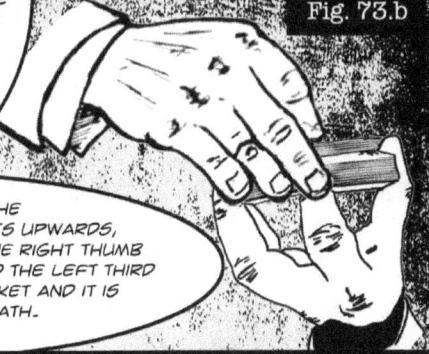

WHEN THE SHIFT IS MASTERED THE ENTIRE ACTION IS ACCOMPLISHED BY A PRESSURE IN OPPOSITE DIRECTIONS ON THE LOWER PACKET, AND THE PACKETS REVERSE **LIKE A FLASH**, BUT OF COURSE IT MUST BE PRACTICED SLOWLY UNTIL THE KNACK IS OBTAINED.

THE POSITIONS OF THE HANDS MAY BE TAKEN WITH EASY DELIBERATION, AS THERE IS NO INDICATION THAT A SHIFT IS MEDITATED.

IT MAY BE MADE WITH THE HANDS STATIONARY WITHOUT EXPOSING THE ACTION.

WITH THE DECK FACE UP IT MAKES AN INSTANTANEOUS "TRANSFORMATION," AND THE POSITION OF THE DECK PERMITS THE OPERATOR TO GET A GLIMPSE OF THE INDEX WITHOUT BEING OBSERVED.

THE SHIFT MAY BE MADE WITH THE RIGHT HAND ALMOST ENTIRELY COVERING THE DECK, BUT THIS ALTERS THE WHOLE CHARACTER AND AIM OF THE PROCESS, THE MAIN ENDEAVOR IS TO MAKE IT AS OPEN AND FREE FROM CONCEALMENT AS POSSIBLE.

THE DIAGONAL PALM-SHIFT.

THE PLAN OF HAVING ONE OR SEVERAL SELECTED CARDS INSERTED IN THE DECK, THEN FORCING THEM THROUGH SLIGHTLY DIAGONALLY, AND TWISTING THEM OUT TO THE TOP OR BOTTOM, IS WELL KNOWN TO MOST CONJURERS, AND BY SOME IS TREATED AS A BLIND SHUFFLE.

THAT THE PROCESS IS NOT SATISFACTORY IS SEEN BY THE FACT THAT IT IS SELDOM OR NEVER EMPLOYED, AND BUT RARELY EVEN MENTIONED IN ANY LIST OF CARD SLIGHTS.

OUR EFFORTS TO IMPROVE, OR RATHER TO COMBINE THE FIRST PART OF THIS MANOEUVRE WITH A PROCESS FOR PALMING THE INSERTED CARDS, INSTEAD OF PLACING THEM ON TOP OR BOTTOM OF THE DECK, IS SHOWN IN THE FOLLOWING DESCRIPTION. THE ACTION IS SILENT, RAPID, UNDETECTABLE IF WELL PERFORMED, AND TAKES PLACE UNDER THE ORDINARY MOVEMENT OF PASSING THE DECK TO BE SHUFFLED.

HOLD THE DECK IN THE LEFT HAND, BY SIDES, BETWEEN THE FIRST JOINTS OF THUMB, AND SECOND, THIRD AND LITTLE FINGERS, FIRST FINGER CURLED UP AT BOTTOM.

ALLOW SPECTATOR TO INSERT SELECTED CARD IN OUTER END OF DECK, PUSHING IT IN UNTIL ABOUT HALF AN INCH ONLY PROTRUDES.

NOW BRING THE RIGHT HAND OVER DECK WITH THE LITTLE FINGER AT SIDE CORNER OF PROTRUDING CARD, SECOND AND THIRD FINGERS AT MIDDLE OF END, AND FIRST FINGER CLOSE TO END CORNER, AND THE THUMB CLOSE TO THE INNER END CORNER OF THE DECK.

APPARENTLY PUSH THE CARD STRAIGHT HOME, BUT REALLY PUSH THE PROTRUDING END WITH THE RIGHT LITTLE FINGER, ABOUT QUARTER OF AN INCH TO THE LEFT, SO THAT THE RIGHT FIRST FINGER CAN PUSH THE TILTED CORNER DOWN THE SIDE OF THE DECK,

THE CARD MOVING SLIGHTLY DIAGONALLY, AND THE OPPOSITE CORNER JUST GRAZING THE RIGHT THUMB, AND PROTRUDING ABOUT THREE-QUARTERS OF AN INCH.

THE LEFT THIRD AND LITTLE FINGERS ARE RELEASED SUFFICIENTLY TO ALLOW THE CARD TO PROTRUDE AT THE SIDE.

THE LEFT THUMB NOW TAKES THE PLACE OF THE RIGHT FIRST FINGER, PUSHING THE CORNER FLUSH WITH SIDE OF DECK. (SEE FIG. 74.)

Fig. 74

THE DIAGONAL POSITION OF THE SELECTED CARD IS NOW PERFECTLY CONCEALED, AND THE DECK IS HELD IN A NATURAL AND REGULAR MANNER.

A LITTLE PRACTICE AT THE DIAGONAL SLIDE ENABLES ONE TO GET THE CARD IN THAT POSITION INSTANTANEOUSLY. THE NEXT ACTION IS TO PALM THE SELECTED CARD IN THE LEFT HAND, AS THE RIGHT PASSES THE DECK TO BE SHUFFLED.

WITH THE LEFT LITTLE FINGER AGAINST THE SIDE OF CARD, SWING OR TURN IT INWARD, USING THE RIGHT THUMB AS A PIVOT, STRAIGHTEN OUT LEFT FIRST, SECOND, AND THIRD FINGERS, CATCHING THE OUTER END AS IT TURNS, AND AT THE SAME TIME SLIDING PACK OUTWARDS AND TO THE RIGHT, THE LEFT HAND TURNING OVER AND INWARDS WITH THE PALMED CARD (SEE FIG. 75)

AND THE LITTLE FINGER SLIPPED TO THE END.

Fig. 75

THERE SHOULD BE NO FORCE OR TWIST EMPLOYED, THE CARD RUNNING OUT AS FREELY AS THOUGH DRAWN. THE CARD AND THE DECK MUST CONTINUE ON THE SAME PLANE UNTIL QUITE FREE OF EACH OTHER.

THE LEFT LITTLE FINGER MAY PRESS THE SIDE OF THE CARD VERY SLIGHTLY UPWARD, SO THAT AS IT IS PALMED IT WILL BEND INTO INSTEAD OF AWAY FROM THE LEFT HAND.

AS THE CARD IS BEING TURNED BY THE LITTLE FINGER THE LEFT THUMB IS RAISED, LETTING THE RIGHT THUMB WITH THE CORNER OF DECK PASS UNDER IT, SO THAT THE CARD CAN LIE PARALLEL WITH, BUT STILL ABOVE, THE LEFT PALM.

AS THE DECK IS SLID OUT, THE RIGHT THUMB SLIDES ALONG THE SIDE OF THE CARD, AND IT IS NOT ACTUALLY PALMED UNTIL THE HANDS ARE ALMOST FREE OF EACH OTHER.

THE WHOLE ACTION MAY BE MADE QUICK AS A FLASH AND WITHOUT A SOUND, YET WHEN PERFORMED QUITE SLOWLY IS STILL A PERFECT BLIND.

THE LEFT HAND MAY SEIZE THE DECK BY THE CORNER, BETWEEN THE FIRST FINGER AND THUMB, AS THE CARD IS PALMED, LEAVING THE RIGHT HAND FREE (SEE FIG. 76).

Fig. 76

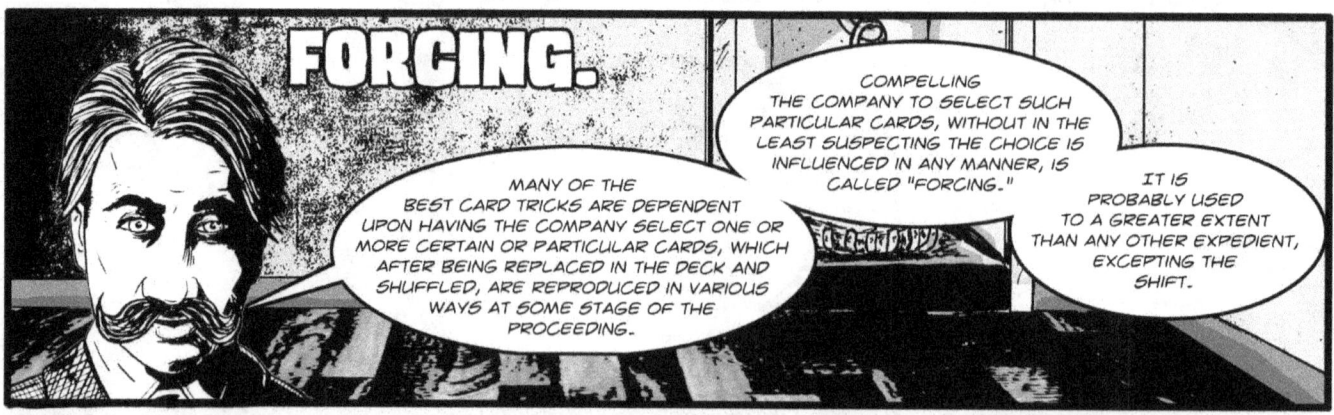

PALMING

IN ADDITION TO THE METHODS GIVEN IN THE FIRST PART OF OUR BOOK, WHICH WE CONSIDER THE BEST FOR GENERAL PURPOSES, WE SHALL DESCRIBE SEVERAL PROCESSES THAT MAY BE EMPLOYED ADVANTAGEOUSLY UNDER SPECIAL CIRCUMSTANCES.

THE TOP CARDS MAY BE PALMED APPARENTLY WITHOUT TOUCHING THE DECK IN THE FOLLOWING MANNER:

HOLD THE DECK ACROSS THE LEFT PALM, THE LITTLE FINGER WELL INSERTED UNDER THE CARDS TO BE PALMED, THE FIRST, SECOND AND THIRD FINGERS HOLDING THE CARDS FIRMLY IN PLACE.

NOW MOVE THE RIGHT HAND, THROUGH SOME NATURAL MOTIVE, OVER THE LEFT, AND AS IT PASSES WITHIN ONE INCH OR TWO STRAIGHTEN OUT THE LEFT-HAND FINGERS, FORCING THE CARDS UP INTO THE RIGHT PALM WITH THE LITTLE FINGER, WHICH IS UNDER THEM.

THE RIGHT HAND EITHER CONTINUES ITS MOVEMENT AS IT SLIGHTLY CLOSES OVER THE PALMED CARDS OR ELSE SEIZES THE DECK IN A MANNER TO EXPOSE IT FULLY, AND THE LEFT HAND MAKES SOME GESTURE OR NATURAL MOVEMENT.

A SIMPLE WAY TO PALM ONE TOP CARD IS TO PUSH IT SLIGHTLY OVER THE SIDE UNDER COVER OF THE RIGHT HAND, THEN PRESS DOWN ON ITS OUTER-END CORNER WITH THE RIGHT LITTLE FINGERTIP, AND IT WILL SPRING UP INTO THE RIGHT PALM.

IN ALL CASES OF PALMING THE DECK SHOULD BE COVERED FOR THE SMALLEST POSSIBLE SPACE OF TIME, AND THE COVERING AND EXPOSING SHOULD BE MADE UNDER SOME NATURAL PRETEXT, SUCH AS SQUARING UP THE CARDS, OR PASSING THE DECK TO THE OTHER HAND, OR CHANGING ITS POSITION IN THE HAND, OR TURNING IT OVER.

THE BACK PALM.

WE ARE AFRAID THE ABOVE TITLE IS A MISNOMER.

THE CARDS TO BE CONCEALED ARE TRANSFERRED TO THE BACK OF THE HAND.

HOLD THE CARD IN THE RIGHT HAND FACE UP BETWEEN THE TIP OF THE THUMB AT ONE END AND TIPS OF SECOND AND THIRD FINGERS AT OPPOSITE END, THE FIRST JOINTS OF THE FIRST AND LITTLE FINGERS HOLD THE SIDES. (SEE FIG. 77.)

Fig. 77

TO MAKE THE "PALM" SLIP THE TIPS OF THE SECOND AND THIRD FINGERS UNDER THE END OF THE CARD AND CURL THEM DOWN UNTIL THEY COME UNDER THE THUMB, AT THE SAME TIME PUSHING THE CARD OUTWARD WITH THE THUMB UNTIL THE INNER CORNERS REACH THE FIRST AND LITTLE FINGERS, WHICH HOLD IT IN POSITION. (SEE FIG. 78.)

Fig. 78

NOW, STRAIGHTEN OUT THE FOUR FINGERS, CLIPPING THE CORNERS OF THE CARD BETWEEN THE LITTLE AND THIRD FINGERTIP'S AND THE FIRST AND SECOND FINGERTIPS, AND THE CARD LIES ALONG THE BACK OF THE HAND. (SEE FIG. 79.)

Fig. 79

TO BRING IT TO THE FRONT AGAIN CURL THE FOUR FINGERS AGAIN INTO THE PALM, STRAIGHTEN THE FIRST FINGERTIP A LITTLE SO THAT THE THUMB MAY TAKE ITS PLACE HOLDING THE CARD, THEN DRAW THE CARD AS FAR AS POSSIBLE TOWARD THE WRIST WITH THE THUMB AND LITTLE FINGER, STRAIGHTENING OUT THE OTHER FINGERS, THEN CLIP THE CORNER BETWEEN THE FIRST AND SECOND FINGERTIPS,

AND SLIDE THE LITTLE FINGER ALONG THE SIDE OF THE CARD UNTIL IT IS STRAIGHT OUT, THIS TIME CLIPPING THE OUTER CORNERS BETWEEN THE SAME FINGERS INSTEAD OF PALMING IN THE USUAL WAY.

SEVERAL CARDS MAY BE TRANSFERRED BACK AND FORTH IN THIS MANNER, AND ONE AT A TIME MAY BE PRODUCED FROM THE BACK WITHOUT SHOWING THE REST.

PERFECTION IN THE FEAT ENABLES A PERFORMER TO SHOW BOTH SIDES OF THE HAND, TRANSFERRING THE CARDS AS IT IS TURNED OVER. A SLIGHT UP-AND-DOWN MOTION AND A BACKWARD TURN OF THE WRIST IS USED.

AS AN EXHIBITION OF DEXTERITY THIS IS PROBABLY UNSURPASSED IN CARD MANIPULATION, BUT IT IS OF LITTLE AID IN THE PERFORMANCE OF TRICKS.

HOWEVER, EVERYTHING MAY BE PUT TO SOME USE, AND THE BACK PALM ONCE HELPED US OUT OF A DIFFICULT SITUATION— "BUT THAT IS ANOTHER STORY."

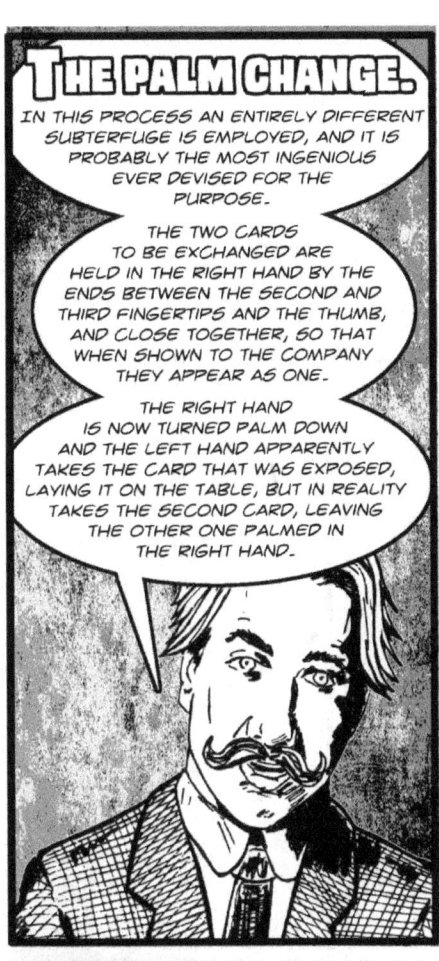

THE PALM CHANGE.

IN THIS PROCESS AN ENTIRELY DIFFERENT SUBTERFUGE IS EMPLOYED, AND IT IS PROBABLY THE MOST INGENIOUS EVER DEVISED FOR THE PURPOSE.

THE TWO CARDS TO BE EXCHANGED ARE HELD IN THE RIGHT HAND BY THE ENDS BETWEEN THE SECOND AND THIRD FINGERTIPS AND THE THUMB, AND CLOSE TOGETHER, SO THAT WHEN SHOWN TO THE COMPANY THEY APPEAR AS ONE.

THE RIGHT HAND IS NOW TURNED PALM DOWN AND THE LEFT HAND APPARENTLY TAKES THE CARD THAT WAS EXPOSED, LAYING IT ON THE TABLE, BUT IN REALITY TAKES THE SECOND CARD, LEAVING THE OTHER ONE PALMED IN THE RIGHT HAND.

THIS IS DONE BY SEIZING BOTH CARDS BETWEEN THE LEFT THUMB AND SECOND AND THIRD FINGERS, AND DRAWING OUT THE UPPER ONE WITH THE THUMB AND PRESSING THE LOWER ONE UP INTO THE RIGHT PALM WITH THE LEFT FINGERS AS THE TOP ONE IS DRAWN OFF. (SEE FIG. 82.)

THIS CHANGE IS ONE OF THE SIMPLEST AND EASIEST FEATS IN THE WHOLE RANGE OF CARD SLIGHTS, AND YET ONE OF THE MOST USEFUL AND UNDETECTABLE. THE ACTION SHOULD BE PERFORMED IN ABOUT THE SAME TIME AND MANNER THAT WOULD ORDINARILY BE TAKEN IN TRANSFERRING A CARD FROM ONE HAND TO THE OTHER.

Fig. 82

THE DOUBLE-PALM CHANGE.

THIS METHOD MAY BE EMPLOYED TO EXCHANGE ONE OR SEVERAL CARDS.

THE CARDS TO BE EXCHANGED LIE IN A PACKET ON THE TABLE FACE UP.

THE OTHER CARDS ARE SECRETLY PALMED FACE DOWN IN THE LEFT HAND.

THE LEFT HAND NOW PICKS UP THE PACKET ON THE TABLE BY THE SIDES, BETWEEN THE THUMB AND SECOND AND THIRD FINGERTIPS, AND TRANSFERS THE PACKET TO THE RIGHT HAND.

AS THE LEFT HAND TURNS PALM UP THE RIGHT HAND PALMS THE PACKET JUST PICKED UP AND SEIZES THE PACKET IN THE LEFT PALM BY THE SIDES, CARRYING IT SLOWLY AND OPENLY AWAY, AND THE LEFT HAND IS SEEN EMPTY. (SEE FIG. 83.)

Fig. 83

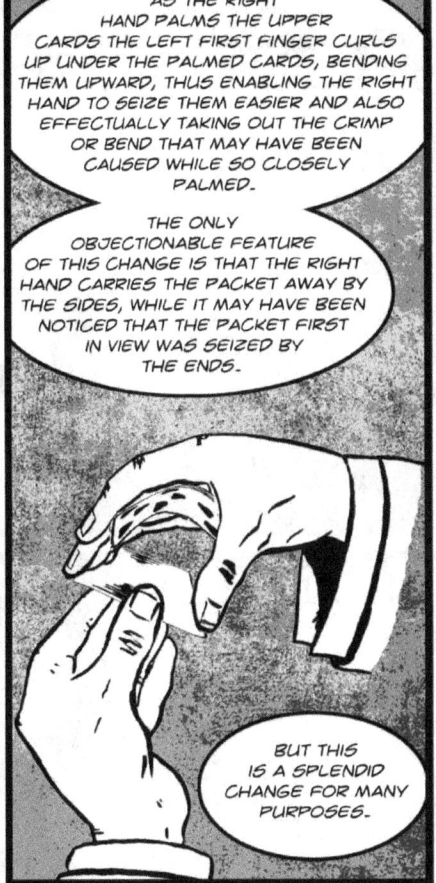

AS THE RIGHT HAND PALMS THE UPPER CARDS THE LEFT FIRST FINGER CURLS UP UNDER THE PALMED CARDS, BENDING THEM UPWARD, THUS ENABLING THE RIGHT HAND TO SEIZE THEM EASIER AND ALSO EFFECTUALLY TAKING OUT THE CRIMP OR BEND THAT MAY HAVE BEEN CAUSED WHILE SO CLOSELY PALMED.

THE ONLY OBJECTIONABLE FEATURE OF THIS CHANGE IS THAT THE RIGHT HAND CARRIES THE PACKET AWAY BY THE SIDES, WHILE IT MAY HAVE BEEN NOTICED THAT THE PACKET FIRST IN VIEW WAS SEIZED BY THE ENDS.

BUT THIS IS A SPLENDID CHANGE FOR MANY PURPOSES.

TRANSFORMATIONS—TWO HANDS

THE CARD CONJURER IN MANY INSTANCES PURPOSELY PRODUCES THE WRONG CARD, AND WHEN HIS ERROR(?) IS PROCLAIMED BY THE COMPANY OR THE INDIVIDUAL, HE COOLLY PROPOSES TO "MAKE GOOD" BY TRANSFORMING THE WRONG CARD INTO THE RIGHT ONE.

THIS IS USUALLY DONE BY PLACING THE WRONG CARD ON THE TOP OR BOTTOM OF THE DECK AND MAKING THE "TRANSFORMATION" WITH THE AID OF BOTH HANDS OR ONLY ONE.

FIRST METHOD.

THE RIGHT HAND HOLDS THE WRONG CARD, WHICH HAS JUST BEEN EXHIBITED; THE LEFT HAND HOLDS THE DECK BETWEEN THE THUMB AND SECOND, THIRD AND LITTLE FINGERS AT THE SIDES, FIRST FINGER AT END, THE BACK OF DECK TO THE PALM AND THE SELECTED CARD ON THE BOTTOM.

THE DECK IS INVERTED OR THE HAND TURNED PALM DOWN, SO THAT THE BOTTOM CARD CANNOT BE SEEN.

THE RIGHT HAND NOW OPENLY PLACES THE WRONG CARD ON THE BOTTOM OF THE DECK AND CARELESSLY SHOWS THE PALM EMPTY.

THEN THE TIPS OF THE RIGHT-HAND FINGERS ARE PLACED AGAINST THE BOTTOM OF THE DECK, BOTH HANDS TURNING IT UP IN VIEW, SHOWING THE WRONG CARD THAT WAS JUST PLACED THERE.

BUT AS THE DECK IS TURNED UP THE RIGHT FINGERTIPS PUSH THE WRONG CARD UP AGAINST THE LEFT FIRST FINGER, ABOUT ONE INCH, SO THAT THE RIGHT PALM A LITTLE BELOW THE BASE OF THE FINGERS MAY BE PRESSED AGAINST THE SELECTED CARD, WHICH IS THE NEXT ONE.

THIS CARD IS DRAWN DOWN SLOWLY BY PRESSING AGAINST IT, THE DOWNWARD MOVEMENT BEING APPARENTLY TO GIVE THE COMPANY A FULL VIEW OF THE WRONG CARD. (SEE FIG. 84.)

Fig. 84

WHEN THE ENDS OF THE TWO CARDS PASS EACH OTHER THE LOWER CARD IS TILTED ON TOP AND THE RIGHT PALM AGAIN COVERS THE WHOLE DECK, CARRYING THE SELECTED CARD ALONG, AND THE LEFT FIRST FINGER PRESSES THE WRONG CARD BACK INTO POSITION.

THE PERFORMER NOW PRONOUNCES THE TALISMANIC WORD, SHOWS THE RIGHT HAND EMPTY, AND THE TRANSFORMATION ACCOMPLISHED.

CLEVERLY EXECUTED, THIS IS A VERY EFFECTIVE SLEIGHT, AND THERE IS LITTLE OR NO DIFFICULTY IN ACQUIRING IT.

IT MAY BE PERFORMED RAPIDLY OR SLOWLY, AS THE OPERATOR FANCIES.

SECOND METHOD

HOLD THE DECK IN THE LEFT HAND, BETWEEN THE THUMB AND SECOND, THIRD AND LITTLE FINGERS, AT SIDES, FIRST FINGERTIP AGAINST THE BACK NEAR END, AND THE BACK, OR TOP CARD, THE SELECTED CARD; THE WRONG CARD BEING ON THE BOTTOM, OR PLACED THERE AND HELD IN FULL VIEW.

TO MAKE THE TRANSFORMATION BRING THE RIGHT HAND OVER THE DECK WITH THE FOUR FINGERTIPS AGAINST THE END.

Fig. 85

SLIDE OR PUSH THE SELECTED CARD WITH THE FIRST FINGERTIP UP AGAINST THE RIGHT-HAND FINGER ENDS, DRAWING THE DECK DOWN TOWARD THE WRIST UNTIL IT CLEARS THE LOWER END OF THE SELECTED CARD, WHICH IS PRESSED INTO THE RIGHT PALM BY THE LEFT FIRST FINGER. (SEE FIG. 85.)

THEN SLIDE THE DECK BACK TO ITS FIRST POSITION.

THIS SLEIGHT MAY BE MADE IN AN INSTANT AND THE ACTION IS FULLY COVERED.

THIRD METHOD.

HOLD THE DECK IN LEFT HAND, RESTING ON ITS SIDE ACROSS THE THIRD JOINTS OF THE FOUR FINGERS, TIP OF THUMB ON TOP SIDE, FACE TO THE COMPANY.

COVER FACE WITH THE RIGHT HAND HELD QUITE FLATLY; TILT TOP SIDE OF DECK SLIGHTLY TOWARD RIGHT HAND; DROP LEFT THUMB TO THE BACK, AND PUSH UP THE TOP CARD.

AS IT COMES ABOVE THE SIDE BRING THE RIGHT-HAND UP AND BACK OVER THE LEFT THUMB, CATCHING THE UP-COMING CARD AGAINST THE SIDE OF THE HAND AND PALMING IT AS IT IS CARRIED OVER, THE LEFT THUMB AIDING THE PALMING BY PRESSING THE CARD HOME.

THE LEFT THUMB THEN INSTANTLY RETAKES ITS POSITION ON THE TOP SIDE OF THE DECK.

THE MOVEMENT OF THE RIGHT HAND IS MADE APPARENTLY TO SHOW THE BOTTOM CARD.

THE RIGHT HAND NOW AGAIN COVERS THE DECK FOR AN INSTANT, LEAVING THE PALMED CARD THERE.

PALMING THE BACK CARD IN THIS MANNER MAY BE DONE VERY RAPIDLY, BUT A SLOW MOVEMENT IS SATISFACTORY.

FOURTH METHOD.

THE ACTION OF THIS TRANSFORMATION IS IDENTICAL WITH THE THIRD METHOD, BUT THE FIRST AND LITTLE FINGERS ARE HELD AGAINST THE ENDS OF THE DECK CLOSE TO THE LOWER CORNERS, THE THUMB AND SECOND AND THIRD FINGERS AT THE TOP AND BOTTOM SIDES AS BEFORE.

IN THIS POSITION THE DECK IS HELD MUCH MORE FIRMLY, AND IT BECOMES EASIER FOR THE LEFT THUMB TO PUSH UP ONE CARD AT A TIME, THE FINGERS AT THE ENDS RESTRAINING THE OTHER CARDS.

THE RIGHT HAND PERFORMS ITS PART AS IN THE THIRD METHOD. THE IMPROVEMENT IS OUR OWN. (SEE FIG. 86.)

Fig. 86

FIFTH METHOD.

HOLD THE DECK IN THE LEFT HAND, THUMB AND THREE FINGERS AT OPPOSITE SIDES, FIRST FINGER AGAINST END.

COVER THE DECK WITH THE RIGHT HAND BUT RUN THE RIGHT THUMB UNDERNEATH.

NOW DRAW OUT THE UNDER CARD WITH THE RIGHT THUMB, PALMING IT,

AND AGAIN COVER THE DECK,

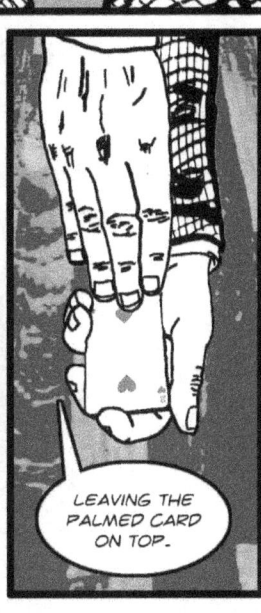

LEAVING THE PALMED CARD ON TOP.

SIXTH METHOD.

NOW WE INTRODUCE ANOTHER "HOMEMADE" ARTICLE, AND CONSEQUENTLY UNKNOWN UP TO THE PRESENT. WE THINK IT IS VERY PRETTY.*

HOLD THE DECK IN THE LEFT HAND BY THE ENDS, BETWEEN THE TIPS OF THE THUMB AND SECOND AND THIRD FINGERS, THE FIRST FINGER RESTING AGAINST THE SIDE AND THE LITTLE FINGERTIP AGAINST THE BOTTOM, CLOSE TO THE CORNER, THE FACE OF THE DECK TO THE COMPANY AND THE FINGER END DOWN.

BRING THE RIGHT HAND FORWARD SO THAT THE LITTLE-FINGERTIPS MEET AT THE CORNER OF DECK, THE PALM PARTLY FACING THE COMPANY AND SHOWING THE HAND EMPTY, THE WRISTS BEING ABOUT SIX INCHES APART.

** THIS IS A ROTATED VERSION OF FIG. 87 THAT MADE IT MUCH EASIER FOR ME TO FIGURE OUT — DT

*WE AGREE! AND THIS ONE IS SUPER FUN TO PRACTICE! — DT

NOW, WITH THE LEFT LITTLE FINGERTIP PUSH THE CORNER OF THE LOWER CARD SLIGHTLY OVER THE SIDE, AND CLIP IT WITH THE RIGHT LITTLE FINGERTIP, SO THAT IT IS FIRMLY HELD BETWEEN THE TWO TIPS (SEE FIG. 87), AND PRESS IT DOWN AGAINST THE LEFT THIRD FINGER, TURNING THE RIGHT HAND OVER AND MOVING THE UPPER END OF THE DECK TO THE LEFT AT THE SAME TIME.

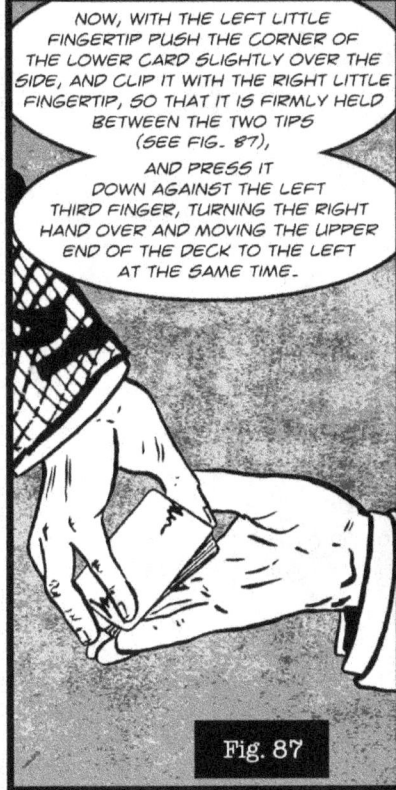

Fig. 87

THIS ACTION WILL CAUSE THE LOWER CARD TO SWING OUT AT THE UPPER END, AND IT IS CAUGHT AND PALMED BY THE RIGHT HAND AS THE HAND TURNS OVER.

THE LEFT LITTLE FINGER IS EXTENDED AS THE TURN IS MADE, PRESSING THE CARD FIRMLY AGAINST THE RIGHT FINGERS. (SEE FIG. 88.)

NOW THE RIGHT HAND IMMEDIATELY SEIZES THE DECK CLOSE TO THE LOWER END, AND THE LEFT HAND RELEASING IT, IS SHOWN EMPTY.

Fig. 88

THEN THE LEFT HAND AGAIN SEIZES THE DECK, BUT THIS TIME BY THE SIDES, WITH THE LITTLE FINGER AGAINST THE LOWER END.

THE RIGHT HAND IS NOW RELEASED AND PASSED RAPIDLY DOWNWARD OVER THE DECK, LEAVING THE PALMED CARD ON TOP, AND THE RIGHT HAND IS SHOWN EMPTY.

THE LEFT LITTLE FINGER AT THE END AIDS THE REPLACING BY CATCHING THE PALMED CARD AS THE RIGHT HAND IS DRAWN DOWN.

OF COURSE, THE PERFORMER MAKES THE MOVEMENTS OF PASSING THE DECK FROM HAND TO HAND AND SHOWING THE HANDS EMPTY, **OSTENSIBLY** TO PROVE THAT NO PALMING TAKES PLACE.

THE ACT OF PALMING, IF CLEVERLY PERFORMED, IS ABSOLUTELY UNDETECTABLE; THE RIGHT HAND TURNING OVER JUST IN TIME AND SUFFICIENTLY TO COVER THE CARD COMING OUT, BUT NOT OBSTRUCTING THE CONTINUED VIEW OF THE FACE OF THE DECK.

THE ACTUAL PALM CAN BE MADE AS RAPIDLY AS DESIRED AND WITHOUT A SOUND.

OUR READERS SHOULD CULTIVATE THIS "TRANSFORMATION," THOUGH IT MAY TAKE SOME LITTLE PRACTICE TO ACQUIRE PERFECTLY.

TRANSFORMATIONS ONE HAND
FIRST METHOD.

HOLD THE DECK IN THE LEFT HAND, THE THUMB WELL EXTENDED ACROSS THE FACE, FIRST FINGER AT END, SECOND AND LITTLE FINGERS AT SIDE AND THIRD FINGER CURLED IN AS FAR AS POSSIBLE UNDERNEATH.

GRIP THE TOP CARD WITH THE THUMB AND DRAW IT BACK, TILTING UP THE DECK WITH THE THIRD FINGER UNTIL THE TOP CARD CLEARS THE SIDE (SEE FIG. 89.),

Fig. 89

Fig. 89.b

THEN PRESS THE TOP CARD DOWN BETWEEN THE CURLED-UP FINGER AND DECK BY BRINGING THE THUMB AGAIN TO ITS ORIGINAL POSITION ACROSS TOP. (SEE FIG. 90.)

THE THIRD AND LITTLE FINGER ENDS STEADY THE PACK AS IT IS TILTED UPWARD, BUT THE FIRST FINGER TAKES NO PART IN THE ACTION.

THE TOP CARD MUST BE GRIPPED WELL INTO THE ROOT OF THE THUMB AND DRAWN BACK AS FAR AS POSSIBLE AS THE DECK IS BEING TILTED UP.

Fig. 90

THE ACTION SHOULD BE COVERED BY A SWING, AND AS IT IS EXTREMELY DIFFICULT TO EXECUTE WITHOUT SOME NOISE THE COMPANY MIGHT BE INFORMED THAT IF THEY CANNOT SEE THE "TRANSFORMATION" THEY WILL BE PERMITTED TO HEAR IT.

THE RAPIDITY OF THE ACTION IS PROPORTIONATE TO THE SKILL OF THE PERFORMER, AND IT MAY BE MADE WITH THE HAND IN **ANY** POSITION.

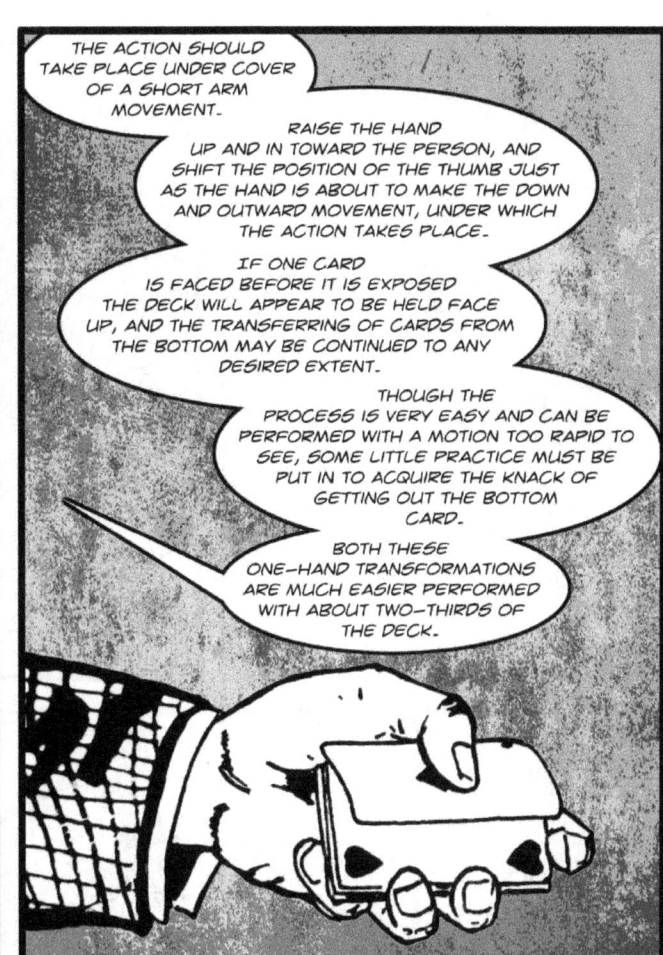

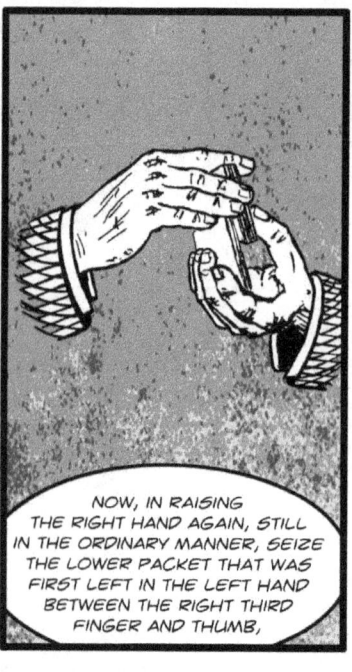
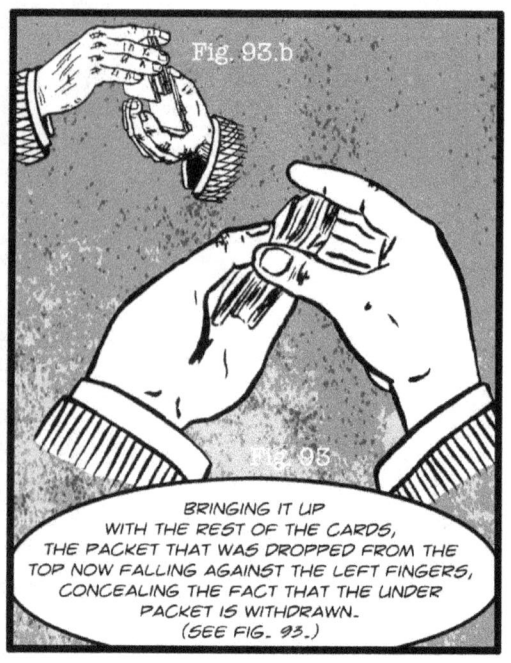
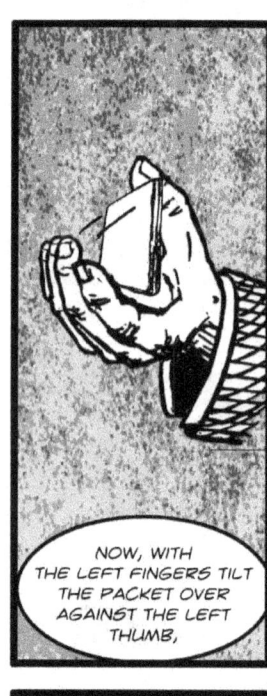

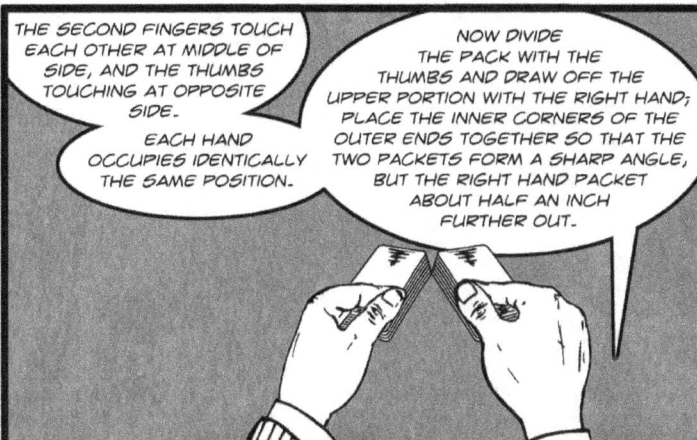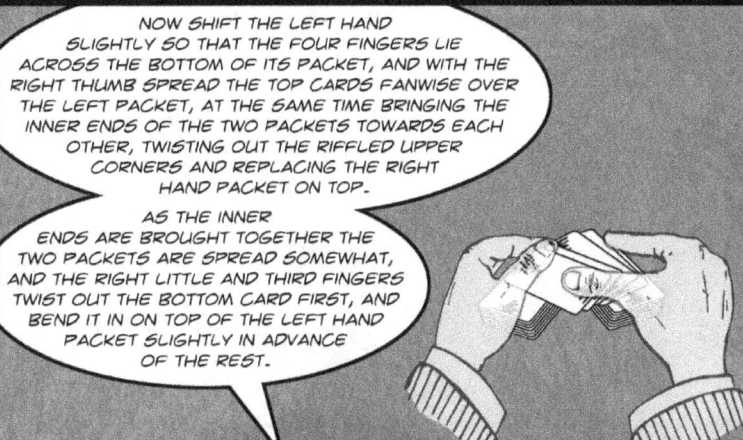

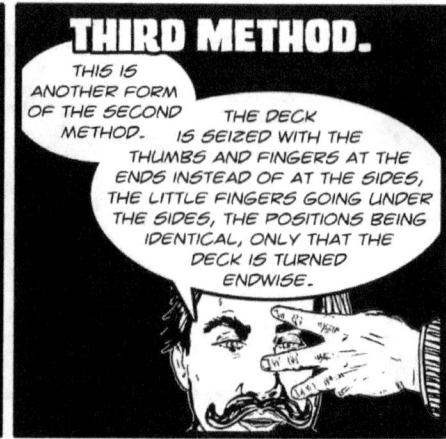

BY SLIGHTLY SPREADING THE TWO PACKETS AS THE SPRINGING OR RIFFLING OF THE SIDES IS CONTINUED THE APPEARANCE OF THE CORNERS BEING INTERLOCKED IS PERFECTLY MAINTAINED.

THIS SHUFFLE CAN BE PERFORMED VERY RAPIDLY, AND WITH PERFECT CONTROL OF THE CARDS, AND IT IS AN EXCELLENT ONE FOR CONJURING, AS THESE PERFORMERS NEVER RIFFLE ON THE TABLE.

BUT, AS WE HAVE MENTIONED, IT IS DIFFICULT, AND IF THE OPERATOR IS NOT A SKILLFUL CARD-HANDLER HE WILL FIND IT QUITE A TASK TO EVEN RIFFLE IN THE TWO PACKETS, AND THIS IS THE SIMPLEST PART OF THE OPERATION.

WHEN THIS RIFFLE IS ALTERNATED WITH THE FOREGOING SHUFFLE IT REQUIRES VERY CLOSE SCRUTINY OF A VERY KNOWING CARD EXPERT TO DETECT THE FACT THAT THE OPERATION IS A BLIND.

THIRD METHOD.

THIS IS ANOTHER FORM OF THE SECOND METHOD.

THE DECK IS SEIZED WITH THE THUMBS AND FINGERS AT THE ENDS INSTEAD OF AT THE SIDES, THE LITTLE FINGERS GOING UNDER THE SIDES, THE POSITIONS BEING IDENTICAL, ONLY THAT THE DECK IS TURNED ENDWISE.

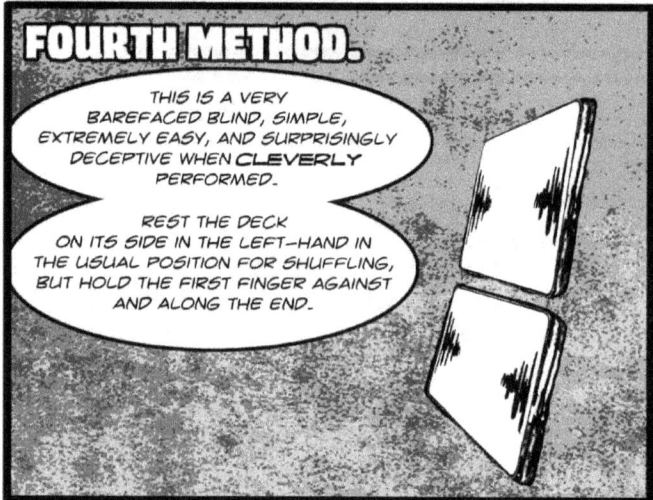

WHEN THE DECK IS SEPARATED INTO THE TWO PACKETS THE THUMBS RIFFLE THE INNER CORNERS TOGETHER, THE LEFT FINGERS ARE SHIFTED ACROSS THE BOTTOM, THE RIGHT THUMB SPREADS THE TOP CARDS OVER THE LEFT-HAND PACKET, AND THE RIGHT HAND BRINGS THE OUTER ENDS OF THE TWO PACKETS TOWARD EACH OTHER, TWISTING OUT THE INTERLOCKED CORNERS AND PLACING THE RIGHT-HAND PACKET AGAIN ON TOP IN MUCH THE SAME MANNER.

IN THIS METHOD THE PACKETS ARE EASIER CONTROLLED, AND IT IS HARD TO SAY WHICH IS THE BETTER.

BUT WE THINK FOR CONJURING PURPOSES THE MORE THE METHODS FOR BLIND SHUFFLING ARE VARIED THE GREATER ARE THE PROBABILITIES OF CONVINCING THE COMPANY THAT THE CARDS ARE GENUINELY MIXED; PROVIDING **ALWAYS**, THAT THE SEVERAL METHODS EMPLOYED APPEAR THE SAME AS THOSE IN COMMON EVERY-DAY USAGE.

FOURTH METHOD.

THIS IS A VERY BAREFACED BLIND, SIMPLE, EXTREMELY EASY, AND SURPRISINGLY DECEPTIVE WHEN **CLEVERLY** PERFORMED.

REST THE DECK ON ITS SIDE IN THE LEFT-HAND IN THE USUAL POSITION FOR SHUFFLING, BUT HOLD THE FIRST FINGER AGAINST AND ALONG THE END.

UNDER-CUT ABOUT HALF THE DECK WITH THE RIGHT HAND, THE FIRST FINGER ON THE TOP SIDE, AND MAKE THE ORDINARY MOVEMENT TO INTERLOCK OR FORCE THE RIGHT-HAND CARDS DOWN AMONG THOSE IN THE LEFT HAND, BRINGING THE SIDES TOGETHER FOR THAT PURPOSE.

ALLOW A FEW OF THE CARDS FROM THE TOP OF THE RIGHT-HAND PACKET TO DROP DOWN ON TOP OF THE OTHER PACKET, BUT PREVENT THEM FROM GOING QUITE TO THE LEFT PALM WITH THE LEFT THUMB.

NOW KEEP UP A CONSTANT LATERAL MOVEMENT WITH THE RIGHT-HAND, SHIFTING THE PACKET RAPIDLY LENGTHWISE ABOUT HALF AN INCH EACH WAY, AS THOUGH FORCING THE TWO PACKETS TO INTERLACE, BUT REALLY DROPPING THE UPPER CARDS ON TOP OF THE LEFT-HAND PACKET, BY HOLDING THE RIGHT-HAND PACKET SLIGHTLY DIAGONALLY OVER THE LOWER ONE, SO THAT THE INNER CORNER OF THE RIGHT HAND PACKET IS JUST OVER THE SIDE OF THE LOWER ONE.

DROP THE TOP CARDS OVER IN THIS MANNER UNTIL ALL ARE APPARENTLY INTERLOCKED ABOUT HALF WAY OR MORE, THEN STRIKE THEM ON THE TOP SIDE WITH THE FINGERS HELD FLATLY, DRIVING THEM DOWN EVEN, AND SQUARE UP THE DECK.

THE FIRST FINGER HELD AGAINST THE END AND THE FIRST OR TOP CARDS OF THE RIGHT-HAND PACKET, GOING OVER IMMEDIATELY AS THE SIDES ARE BROUGHT TOGETHER, EFFECTUALLY CONCEAL THE RUSE.

IF THE PROCESS OF ACTUALLY INTERLOCKING THE CARDS IS TRIED IT WILL BE SEEN HOW PERFECTLY THE ACTION CAN BE IMITATED.

AN OCCASIONAL CUT TENDS TO INCREASE THE DECEPTION.

FIFTH METHOD.

THIS PROCESS IS VERY MUCH EMPLOYED BY MANY CLEVER CARD CONJURERS WHO OUGHT TO KNOW BETTER, AND WE INCLUDE IT ONLY BECAUSE IT IS IN COMMON USE AND TO **SUGGEST ITS REJECTION**.

IT CONSISTS IN PUSHING SMALL PACKETS ALTERNATELY FROM THE TOP AND BOTTOM OF THE PORTION HELD IN ONE HAND TO THE BOTTOM AND TOP OF THE PORTION HELD IN THE OTHER.

THE DECK IS HELD IN THE LEFT HAND AND SEVERAL CARDS ARE PUSHED OVER BY THE LEFT THUMB INTO THE RIGHT HAND.

THEN THE LEFT FINGERS PUSH SEVERAL CARDS FROM THE BOTTOM ON TOP OF THE RIGHT-HAND CARDS.

THEN THE LEFT THUMB AGAIN PUSHES SEVERAL FROM THE TOP, BUT THESE ARE RECEIVED UNDER THE RIGHT-HAND PORTION. THE LEFT FINGERS NOW PUSH SEVERAL FROM THE BOTTOM TO THE TOP OF THE RIGHT-HAND PORTION, AND SO ON UNTIL THE LEFT HAND IS EMPTY.

THIS CLUMSY JUGGLING MIGHT PROVE SATISFACTORY IF PERFORMED BY AN AWKWARD NOVICE BEFORE A PARCEL OF SCHOOL CHILDREN, BUT IT APPEARS **SIMPLY RIDICULOUS** IN THE HANDS OF A CARD CONJURER, WHO, IT IS PRESUMED, KNOWS HOW TO SHUFFLE A DECK IN THE CUSTOMARY MANNER, AND WITH AT LEAST THE DEGREE OF SMOOTHNESS THAT ANY ORDINARY PERSON MIGHT POSSESS.

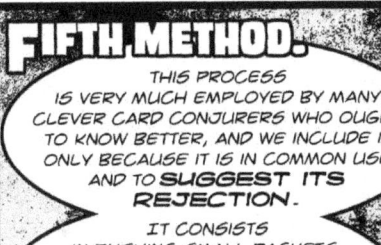

METHODS FOR DETERMINING A CARD THOUGHT OF

IN THREE OF THE FOLLOWING INSTANCES THE SPECTATOR HAS NO CHOICE, AS HE IS SUPPOSED TO THINK OF A CARD HE SEES, AND THE PERFORMER SHOWS HIM BUT ONE, THOUGH APPARENTLY WITHOUT DESIGN.

IN THE FOURTH INSTANCE A MOST INGENIOUS RUSE IS EMPLOYED, THE SPECTATOR BEING GIVEN PERFECT FREEDOM, YET THE CARD IS DETERMINED ALMOST AS SURELY.

A. HOLD THE DECK IN THE LEFT HAND, THUMB ACROSS TOP NEAR INNER END, AND FIRST AND SECOND FINGERS AT SIDE.

BRING OVER THE RIGHT HAND AND SEIZE DECK WITH FINGERS AT OUTER ENDS, THUMB AT INNER END, AND HOLD SO THAT THE OUTER ENDS OF THE CARDS MAY BE SPRUNG OR "RUFFLED," WITH THE FACES TOWARDS THE SPECTATOR.

REQUESTING HIM TO THINK OF A CARD, SPRING THE ENDS RAPIDLY, STOPPING FOR AN INSTANT AT ANY ONE PLACE (SEE FIG. 95), THEN COMPLETING THE RUFFLE.

THE SPRINGING IS PERFORMED AT SUCH A PACE THAT THE SPECTATOR CAN RECOGNIZE BUT ONE CARD, WHICH IS MORE FULLY EXPOSED BY THE MOMENTARY LULL IN THE SPRINGING, AND AT THIS POINT THE PERFORMER FORMS AND HOLDS A BREAK WITH END OF LEFT SECOND FINGER.

AT THE END OF THE FIRST RUFFLE ASK IF CARD HAS BEEN NOTED, AND IF NOT REPEAT THE ACTION, BUT OF COURSE HESITATING AT SOME OTHER POINT.

Fig. 95

B. HOLD THE DECK LENGTHWISE IN THE RIGHT HAND, FACE TO PALM, BETWEEN SECOND JOINT OF THUMB AND ENDS OF FINGERS.

BEND FINGER END DOWNWARDS AND ALLOW ENDS TO ESCAPE RAPIDLY, SPRINGING THEM INTO THE LEFT HAND IN THE USUAL MANNER OF THE FLOURISH.

OF COURSE THE PERFORMER CONCEALS HIS NOTICE OF THE CARDS AS FAR AS POSSIBLE.

HESITATE, OR STOP THE SPRINGING FOR AN INSTANT, AT ANY STAGE OF THE OPERATION (SEE FIG. 96), AND THE ONLY CARD THAT THE PERFORMER CAN NOTICE OR FAIRLY DISTINGUISH WILL BE THE PROBABLE SELECTION OF THE SPECTATOR.

Fig. 96

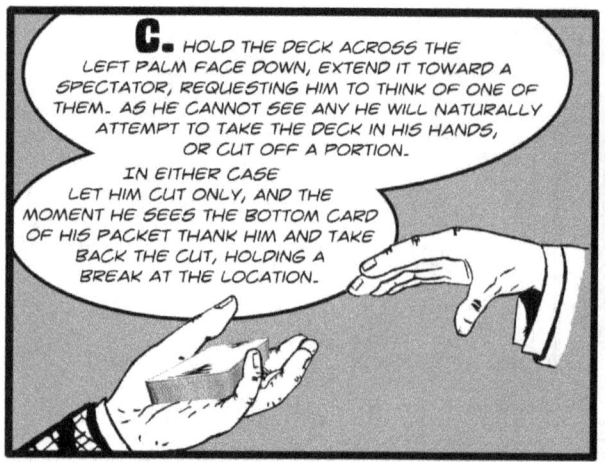

C. Hold the deck across the left palm face down, extend it toward a spectator, requesting him to think of one of them. As he cannot see any he will naturally attempt to take the deck in his hands, or cut off a portion.

In either case let him cut only, and the moment he sees the bottom card of his packet thank him and take back the cut, holding a break at the location.

D. This cunning and absolutely **UNFATHOMABLE STRATAGEM** must have been devised by an individual of truly Machiavelian subtlety.

The deck is held in the left-hand face down and the cards are taken off in the right hand and held face to the spectator.

Each card is counted as it is taken off the deck, and the right-hand packet is kept well squared up, so that but one card remains exposed to view.

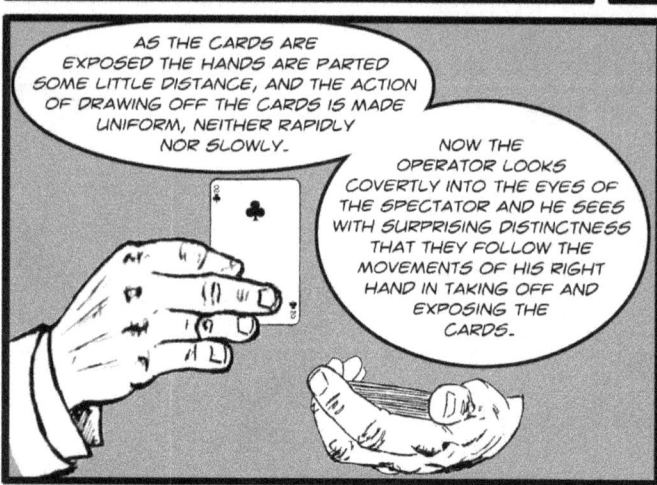

As the cards are exposed the hands are parted some little distance, and the action of drawing off the cards is made uniform, neither rapidly nor slowly.

Now the operator looks covertly into the eyes of the spectator and he sees with surprising distinctness that they follow the movements of his right hand in taking off and exposing the cards.

The moment the eyes rest, or lose their intensity, the performer notes the number of the card, but continues the drawing off process.

Shortly, asking if a card has been thought of, he closes up deck, secretively counts off to the number, and produces at will.

Of course a break may be held at the card noted, but the counting avoids the least change in the right-hand action.

TO GET SIGHT OF SELECTED CARD

A simple plan of catching a glimpse of a selected card is to have it inserted at the end and prevent the spectator from pushing it quite home by squeezing the deck.

Then, with the card protruding about a quarter of an inch, covertly turn the deck partially over by passing it to the other hand, and get sight of the index.

Another and better plan is to push the selected card through diagonally, and square up, leaving it protruding at the inner end. In this case the index is at the diagonal corner and more easily seen, and the fact of the card protruding can be covered completely.

Still another plan is to insert the left little finger under the inserted card and slightly tilt up inner left-hand corner to note the index.

THE SLIDE

Hold the deck in the left hand, back to palm, fingers and thumb at opposite sides.

Show face of deck to company, then turn it down, and with tips of third and little fingers slide the bottom card half an inch or so towards wrist (see Fig. 97), and draw the next card out at end with right-hand fingers.

Of course this has the appearance of drawing off the card just shown to the company.

It is a form of exchange that may be occasionally employed.

Fig. 97

FAVORITE SLEIGHTS FOR TERMINATING TRICKS

CATCHING TWO CARDS AT FINGERTIPS

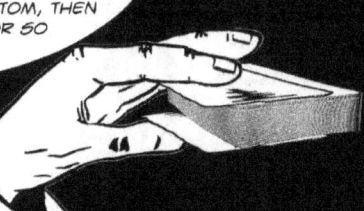

A FAVORITE MANNER OF TERMINATING A TRICK THAT REQUIRES THE PRODUCTION OF TWO SELECTED CARDS IS TO BRING ONE TO TOP AND ONE TO BOTTOM, THEN TOSS THE DECK IN THE AIR A YARD OR SO STRAIGHT UPWARD,

RETAINING THE TOP AND BOTTOM CARDS BY PRESSURE AND FRICTION OF THUMB AND FINGERS, THEN THRUSTING THE HAND AMONG THE CARDS AS THEY DESCEND, APPARENTLY FINDING THE SELECTED CARDS IN THE ACT.

LEAVING SELECTED CARD IN HAND OF SPECTATOR.

A PLAN FOR THE PRODUCTION OF A SINGLE CARD, AS, THE LAST OF A SERIES, IS TO BRING IT TO THE BOTTOM FACE UP AND REQUEST A SPECTATOR TO HOLD THE DECK FIRMLY BY THE CORNER, THUMB ON TOP.

BY STRIKING THE DECK FORCIBLY FROM ABOVE ALL THE CARDS, WILL FALL FROM HIS HAND SAVE THE SELECTED CARD, WHICH IS RETAINED BY THE FRICTION OF THE FINGERS AND LEFT FACE UP IN HIS HAND.

THE REVOLUTION.

THIS IS A GREAT FAVORITE FOR TERMINATING CERTAIN TRICKS, AND HAS A VERY SHOWY APPEARANCE.

IF THE TOP CARD IS PUSHED OVER THE SIDE ABOUT HALF AN INCH, AND THE DECK DROPPED FLATLY ON THE TABLE FROM A POINT OF PERHAPS TWELVE OR FIFTEEN INCHES ABOVE IT, THE TOP CARD WILL TURN OVER IN THE DESCENT AND LIE FAIRLY ON TOP OF THE DECK, FACE EXPOSED.

THE TURN IS CAUSED BY THE RESISTANCE OF THE AIR AGAINST THE PROTRUDING SIDE.

THE FACTS THAT THE CARD TO BE PRODUCED IS ON TOP, AND THAT A CARD IS PUSHED OVER, ARE CONCEALED.

CARDS RISING FROM THE HAND.

THE SELECTED CARDS ARE BROUGHT TO TOP OF DECK AND THE PACK IS HELD IN THE LEFT HAND, THUMB AT ONE SIDE AND LYING STRAIGHT ALONG WITH TIP NEAR END, SECOND THIRD AND LITTLE FINGERS AT OPPOSITE SIDE, AND FIRST FINGER AT BACK.

THE CARDS ARE PUSHED UP BY FIRST FINGER, THE THUMB AND OTHER FINGERS BEING RELEASED SUFFICIENTLY TO ALLOW THEIR RISING, BUT RETAINING THEIR POSITION. (SEE FIG. 98.)

WHEN THE CARDS ARE RAISED TO NEARLY THE FULL LENGTH THE RIGHT HAND TAKES THEM OFF.

SOME ADDRESS IS NECESSARY TO PUSH UP A CARD WITH ONE FINGER, BUT A LITTLE PRACTICE, AND ESPECIALLY AT THE MANNER OF HOLDING THE DECK, SO AS TO KEEP THE CARD IN POSITION AND YET NOT RETARD ITS UPWARD COURSE, WILL SOON ACQUIRE THE ABILITY.

IF THE FIRST AND SECOND FINGERS ARE PLACED AT THE BACK THE FEAT BECOMES MUCH EASIER, BUT OF COURSE THE EFFECT IS PROPORTIONATELY LESSENED.

Fig. 98

CARD TRICKS EXPLANATORY

IT IS NOT OUR PURPOSE TO DESCRIBE THE VARIOUS KINDS OF APPARATUS, OR PREPARED OR MECHANICAL CARDS, THAT PLAY SO GREAT A PART IN THE PROFESSIONAL CONJURER'S STARTLING EXHIBITIONS.

THE ENUMERATION ALONE OF THESE DEVICES WOULD FILL A VOLUME TWICE THIS SIZE; AND ANYWAY THEY WOULD BE OF LITTLE SERVICE TO THE AMATEUR FOR IMPROMPTU ENTERTAINMENT.

BUT WE SHALL DESCRIBE SOME TRICKS THAT MAY BE PERFORMED WITH AN ORDINARY DECK, UNDER ANY CIRCUMSTANCES, PROVIDING THE NECESSARY SKILL HAS BEEN ACQUIRED TO EXECUTE THE SLEIGHTS.

HOWEVER, THE ARTIST WHO HAS ATTAINED SOME DEGREE OF PROFICIENCY IN MANIPULATION AS TAUGHT BY THIS WORK, MAY BY TAXING HIS WITS A LITTLE, DEVISE NO END OF TRICKS FOR HIMSELF, WITH THE ADVANTAGE THAT THEY WILL NOT BE "SHOP WORN" ARTICLES.

THE SIMPLEST SLEIGHT, IF WELL RIGGED UP WITH EITHER PLAUSIBLE OR NONSENSICAL CLAP-TRAP, MAY BE MADE TO PROVIDE A MOST ASTONISHING AND ELABORATE CARD TRICK;

WHEREAS, IF THE SLEIGHT BE EXHIBITED ALONE, THE EFFECT IS NOT AT ALL COMMENSURATE WITH THE TIME AND LABOR SPENT IN ACQUIRING THE SKILL.

CONCEAL, AS FAR AS POSSIBLE, THE POSSESSION OF DIGITAL ABILITY, AND LEAVE THE COMPANY STILL GUESSING HOW IT IS DONE.

FOR SOME OF THE FOLLOWING TRICKS WE HAVE INVENTED NAMES AND GARNISHED THEM UP WITH A RIGMAROLE MERELY TO SHOW THE PART THAT "PATTER" PLAYS IN CARD ENTERTAINMENTS.

OUR READERS ESSAYING THE TRICKS SHOULD COMPOSE THEIR OWN MONOLOGUE, SO THAT IT MAY BE IN KEEPING WITH THEIR PARTICULAR PERSONALITY OR STYLE OF ADDRESS.

THE EXCLUSIVE COTERIE.

IN EFFECT:
THE FOUR QUEENS ARE SELECTED AND LAID FACE DOWN IN A ROW ON THE TABLE. THREE INDIFFERENT CARDS ARE PLACED ON EACH QUEEN. NOW THE COMPANY SELECTS ONE OF THE FOUR PACKETS, AND IT IS FOUND TO CONSIST OF THE FOUR QUEENS ONLY.

SLEIGHTS: PALM AND SHIFT

PATTER AND EXECUTION:

"LADIES AND GENTLEMEN, I SHALL ENDEAVOR TO ILLUSTRATE, WITH THE AID OF THIS ORDINARY DECK OF CARDS, HOW FUTILE ARE THE EFFORTS OF PLEBEIANS TO BREAK INTO THAT SELECT CIRCLE OF SOCIETY KNOWN AS THE BEAU-MONDE*,

AND ESPECIALLY HOW SUCH ENTREE IS PREVENTED BY THE POLITE BUT FRIGID EXCLUSIVENESS OF ITS GENTLER MEMBERS.

*FASHIONABLE SOCIETY--DT

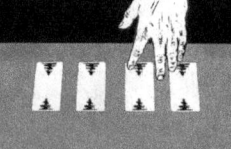

"WE SHALL ASSUME THAT IT IS THE OCCASION OF A PUBLIC RECEPTION, OUR TABLE THE HALL, OUR DECK THE COMMON HERD, AND WE MAY FITTINGLY SELECT THE FOUR QUEENS AS REPRESENTING THE FEMININE PORTION OF THE SMART SET."

(LAY FOUR QUEENS FACE DOWN ON TABLE.)

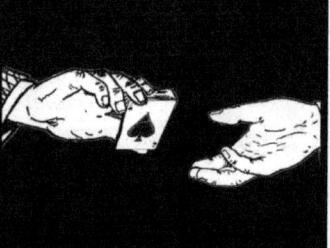

"WILL SOME ONE NOW KINDLY SEE THAT THERE ARE NO MORE QUEENS IN THE DECK."

(HAND DECK FOR INSPECTION.)

"THERE ARE NO MORE QUEENS IN THE DECK? THANKS!"

(TAKE DECK BACK.)

"BUT ARE WE ALL QUITE SURE THAT THE CARDS ON THE TABLE ARE THE FOUR QUEENS? PLEASE EXAMINE THEM."

(HAND THEM TO ONE OF THE COMPANY, AND NOW SECRETLY PALM THREE CARDS IN RIGHT HAND.)

"THEY ARE THE FOUR QUEENS? KINDLY PLACE THEM ON THE DECK."

(EXTEND DECK IN LEFT HAND AND WHEN QUEENS ARE PLACED ON TOP SECRETLY PLACE PALMED CARDS ON TOP OF THEM.)

"NOW, AS OUR TABLE IS SUPPOSED TO BE THE SCENE OF THIS GRAND FUNCTION, WE SHALL STATION THOSE FOUR PARTICULARLY EXCLUSIVE LADIES AT DIFFERENT POINTS IN THE ROOM"

(LAY OUT THE FIRST THREE TOP CARDS FACE DOWN),

"GIVING HER MAJESTY THE QUEEN OF ——"

(HESITATE AND CARELESSLY TURN QUEEN FACE UP APPARENTLY TO SEE THE SUIT, AND ALLOW THE COMPANY TO SEE IT ALSO, THEN NAME THE SUIT),

THE INVISIBLE FLIGHT.

IN EFFECT. A CARD IS SELECTED BY THE COMPANY. THE PERFORMER PLACES IT ON THE TABLE TO THE RIGHT. ANOTHER CARD IS SELECTED AND PERFORMER PLACES IT ON TABLE TO THE LEFT. THE FIRST DRAWN CARD IS NOW PLACED ON TOP OF THE DECK, WHICH WAS LYING ON THE TABLE, AND THE TWO SELECTED CARDS ARE COMMANDED TO CHANGE PLACES AND FOUND TO HAVE DONE SO.

SLEIGHTS:
TOP CHANGE AND PALM CHANGE.

EXECUTION:
STAND BEHIND THE TABLE FACING THE COMPANY.

HAVE A CARD SELECTED BY A SPECTATOR TO THE RIGHT, HOLD DECK IN LEFT HAND, TAKE BACK DRAWN CARD IN RIGHT HAND, SHOW IT FIRST TO THE COMPANY ON THE RIGHT, THEN TO COMPANY ON THE LEFT, THEN EXCHANGE IT FOR TOP CARD OF DECK WHEN MAKING HALF TURN AGAIN TO THE RIGHT AND DEPOSIT CARD WITH SAME MOVEMENT ON THE TABLE AT THE RIGHT SIDE.

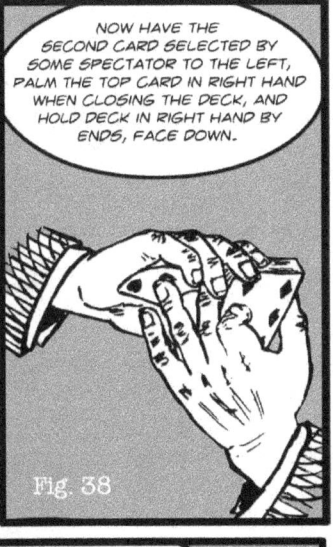
NOW HAVE THE SECOND CARD SELECTED BY SOME SPECTATOR TO THE LEFT, PALM THE TOP CARD IN RIGHT HAND WHEN CLOSING THE DECK, AND HOLD DECK IN RIGHT HAND BY ENDS, FACE DOWN.

Fig. 38

TAKE BACK SECOND DRAWN CARD IN LEFT HAND, SHOWING IT TO COMPANY ON LEFT.

NOW DROP DECK ON MIDDLE OF TABLE, AND TAKE SECOND SELECTED CARD FROM THE LEFT HAND INTO THE RIGHT, SEIZING IT BY THE ENDS, AND DEPOSITING PALMED CARD ON TOP OF IT.

HOLD CLOSELY TOGETHER AND SHOW AS ONE CARD TO COMPANY ON THE RIGHT.

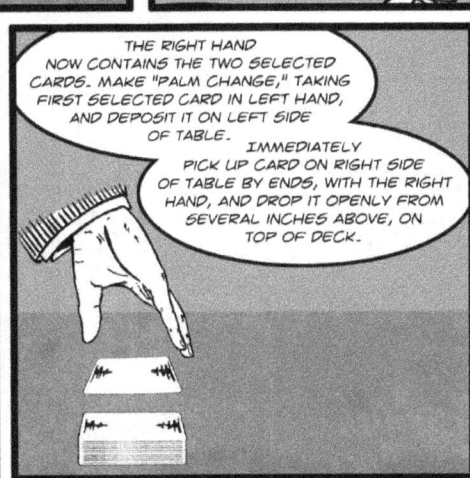
THE RIGHT HAND NOW CONTAINS THE TWO SELECTED CARDS. MAKE "PALM CHANGE," TAKING FIRST SELECTED CARD IN LEFT HAND, AND DEPOSIT IT ON LEFT SIDE OF TABLE.

IMMEDIATELY PICK UP CARD ON RIGHT SIDE OF TABLE BY ENDS, WITH THE RIGHT HAND, AND DROP IT OPENLY FROM SEVERAL INCHES ABOVE, ON TOP OF DECK.

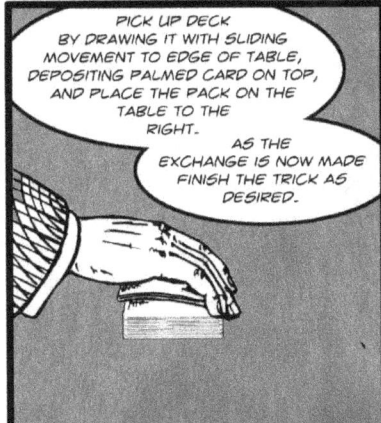
PICK UP DECK BY DRAWING IT WITH SLIDING MOVEMENT TO EDGE OF TABLE, DEPOSITING PALMED CARD ON TOP, AND PLACE THE PACK ON THE TABLE TO THE RIGHT.

AS THE EXCHANGE IS NOW MADE FINISH THE TRICK AS DESIRED.

THE FIRST EXCHANGE IS MADE BY EMPLOYING THE "TOP CHANGE," AND THE TACIT EXCUSE FOR BRINGING THE HANDS TOGETHER FOR THE INSTANT IS OBTAINED BY SHOWING THE CARD FIRST TO THE COMPANY ON THE RIGHT, THEN TO THE LEFT, AND THEN DEPOSITING THE CARD ON RIGHT SIDE OF TABLE.

Fig. 80

THE SECOND EXCHANGE IS MADE VERY SLOWLY, OR AT LEAST IN THE USUAL TIME REQUIRED TO PASS A CARD FROM ONE HAND TO THE OTHER. THE ENTIRE COMPANY SHOULD BE PERMITTED TO SEE THE CARD ABOUT TO BE PALMED; THEN THE HAND IS NATURALLY TURNED DOWN AS THE LEFT FINGERS APPARENTLY CARRY AWAY TO THE LEFT THE CARD JUST SHOWN.

WHEN THE TABLE CARD IS DROPPED ON THE DECK, IT MAY BE PERMITTED TO FALL UNEVENLY, GIVING ONE REASON FOR PICKING UP THE DECK, I. E., TO SQUARE UP. TRANSFERRING THE DECK FROM THE MIDDLE OF THE TABLE TO THE RIGHT SIDE IS THE SECOND TACIT EXCUSE.

THIS TRICK IS USUALLY PERFORMED BY HAVING ONE DUPLICATE CARD, AND FORCING IT, IN WHICH CASE THE ASSISTANCE OF THE DECK FOR THE THIRD EXCHANGE IS NOT REQUIRED.

BUT AS WE CONFINE OUR LIST TO THOSE THAT MAY BE PERFORMED WITH AN ORDINARY DECK, THE FOREGOING METHOD WILL BE FOUND SATISFACTORY.

TRICKS WITH THE PREARRANGED DECK

THE USUAL PLAN IS TO ARRANGE THE WHOLE PACK IN THE ORDER SUGGESTED BY THE FOLLOWING JINGLE, VIZ.:

"EIGHT KINGS THREATENED TO SAVE NINETY-FIVE QUEENS FROM ONE SICK KNAVE."

THUS INDICATING THE ORDER OF THE THIRTEEN VALUES, AS EIGHT, KING, THREE, TEN, TWO, SEVEN, NINE, FIVE, QUEEN, FOUR, ACE, SIX, JACK.

8 KINGS THREATEN TO SAVE NINETY-FIVE QUEENS FROM ONE SICK KNAVE.
8 KING THREE TEN TWO SEVEN NINE FIVE QUEEN FOUR ACE SIX JACK.

THE SUITS ARE TAKEN IN A REGULAR ORDER, SAY, DIAMONDS, CLUBS, HEARTS, SPADES.

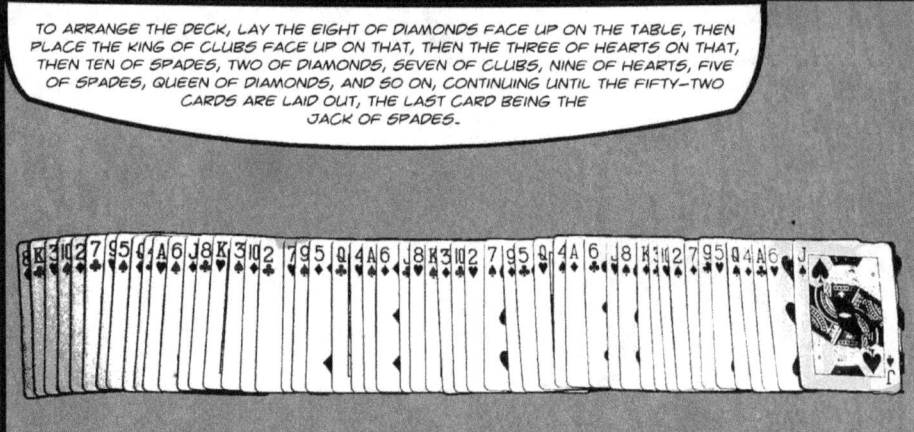

TO ARRANGE THE DECK, LAY THE EIGHT OF DIAMONDS FACE UP ON THE TABLE, THEN PLACE THE KING OF CLUBS FACE UP ON THAT, THEN THE THREE OF HEARTS ON THAT, THEN TEN OF SPADES, TWO OF DIAMONDS, SEVEN OF CLUBS, NINE OF HEARTS, FIVE OF SPADES, QUEEN OF DIAMONDS, AND SO ON, CONTINUING UNTIL THE FIFTY-TWO CARDS ARE LAID OUT, THE LAST CARD BEING THE JACK OF SPADES.

SIR, I'M PRETTY SURE THE GUY WHO MADE THIS HAS WORKED ON SOME MEMORY BOOKS TOO! HE'S A BIT ECCENTRIC, TO PUT IT NICELY, BUT IN THE FUTURE, PEOPLE CALL HIS WORK "DA BOMB."

OBVIOUSLY THIS WASN'T IN THE ORIGINAL, OR ANY OF THE REPRINTS, BUT IT IS NOW! SNOOCHIES! – DAPPER D

ANY ARRANGEMENT IS AS GOOD AS ANOTHER SO LONG AS THE VALUES DO NOT RUN IN THEIR REGULAR ORDER, I. E., ONE, TWO, THREE, FOUR, FIVE, ETC., AND THOUGH THE ABOVE ARRANGEMENT IS WELL KNOWN, IT DOES NOT MATTER IN THE LEAST WHEN PERFORMING.

ONLY THOSE WHO ARE WELL VERSED IN CARD TRICKS WOULD RECOGNIZE THE ORDER, AND SUCH PERSONS CANNOT BE DECEIVED WITH ANY KIND OF ARRANGEMENT.

THE TAX ON THE MEMORY IS VERY SLIGHT, THERE BEING BUT THIRTEEN NAMES TO COMMIT, AND CONNING THEM OVER FOR HALF AN HOUR OR SO SHOULD IMPRESS THEIR ORDER ON THE MIND PERMANENTLY.

THE DECK SO ARRANGED MAKES EVERY THIRTEENTH CARD THE SAME VALUE, AND OF THE NEXT SUIT IN THE ORDER OF SUITS; EVERY FOURTH CARD THE SAME SUIT, AND EVERY SECOND CARD THE OTHER SUIT OF THE SAME COLOR.

CUTTING DOES NOT DISTURB THE ORDER AND THE TOP CARD IS ALWAYS NEXT IN THE REGULAR ORDER TO THE BOTTOM, AND THE PERFORMER, SECRETLY NOTING THE BOTTOM CARD, HAS THE KEY TO THE SITUATION.

WE SHALL DESCRIBE SEVERAL VERY STARTLING EFFECTS THAT MAY BE CAUSED BY THE EMPLOYMENT OF THE PREARRANGED DECK IN THE HANDS OF A REALLY CLEVER OPERATOR.

OF COURSE, THE PREARRANGEMENT MUST BE CAREFULLY CONCEALED.

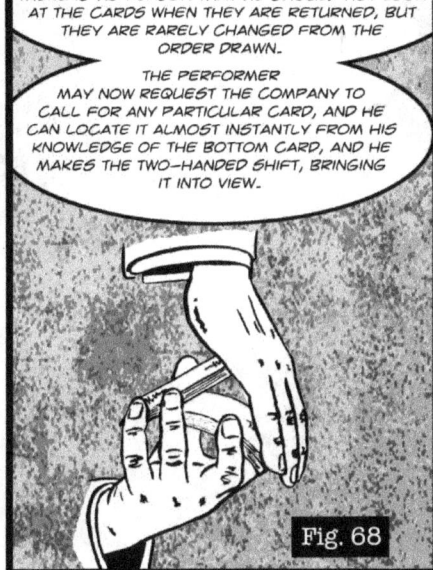

THE CARD CONJURER'S REPERTORY IS NEVER COMPLETE WITHOUT EMPLOYING THE PREARRANGED DECK TO SOME EXTENT, AND WE BELIEVE THE RULES HERE GIVEN FOR DETERMINING THE CARD AT ANY NUMBER GIVEN, AND THE NUMBER OF ANY CARD CALLED FOR, ARE THE FIRST EVER FORMULATED FOR A FIFTY-TWO-CARD DECK.

THE TRAVELING CARDS.

IN EFFECT: A CARD IS SELECTED AND REPLACED IN THE DECK, WHICH IS THEN THOROUGHLY SHUFFLED. PERFORMER NOW CAUSES THE CARDS TO FLY UP HIS SLEEVE, ONE, TWO, OR SEVERAL AT A TIME, PRODUCING THEM FROM THE SHOULDER. THE SELECTED CARD IS CALLED UPON TO LEAVE THE DECK AT THE COMPANY'S DESIRE, AND THE OPERATION IS CONTINUED UNTIL THE LAST SEVERAL CARDS, WHICH ARE NOTED, DISAPPEAR FROM THE HAND AND ARE SLOWLY PRODUCED FROM THE SHOULDER.

SLEIGHTS: MASTERLY FEATS OF PALMING AND UNFLINCHING AUDACITY.

EXECUTION AND PATTER: "LADIES AND GENTLEMEN: I AM CONSTANTLY IMPORTUNED BY SOME OF THE MOST CURIOUS AND LEAST DISCERNING OF MY AUDITORS TO EXPLAIN THE MANNER BY WHICH THE RESULTS IN CERTAIN TRICKS ARE ACHIEVED.

WHILE I CONSIDER IT UNPROFESSIONAL TO MAKE THESE DISCLOSURES, I ACCEDE SOMEWHAT TO THE PREVALENT DEMAND, AND TO-NIGHT I AM GOING TO TAKE YOU ESPECIALLY INTO MY CONFIDENCE AND EXPOSE ONE OF THE MOST IMPORTANT SECRETS IN THE WHOLE REALM OF CONJURING.

ALTHOUGH MANY PROFESSORS OF THE ART VEHEMENTLY DENY THE IMPUTATION, IT IS NEVERTHELESS A FACT THAT THE COAT SLEEVE OF THE MAGICIAN IS TO HIM MUCH THE SAME AS A SARATOGA TRUNK TO A SUMMER GIRL.

WHERE DOES HE GET HIS BOUQUETS OF ROSES, BASKETS OF EGGS, DISHES OF SWIMMING FISHES? 'UP HIS SLEEVE.'

HOW DO HIS RABBITS, BIRD CAGES AND CANNON BALLS DISAPPEAR? 'UP HIS SLEEVE.' THE SAYING IS AS TRUE AS IT IS ANCIENT, AND I SHALL PROVE MY ASSERTIONS BY DEMONSTRATING THE PROCESS; AND THOUGH YOU MAY DOUBT MY VERACITY, YOU CERTAINLY CANNOT QUESTION YOUR OWN EYES.

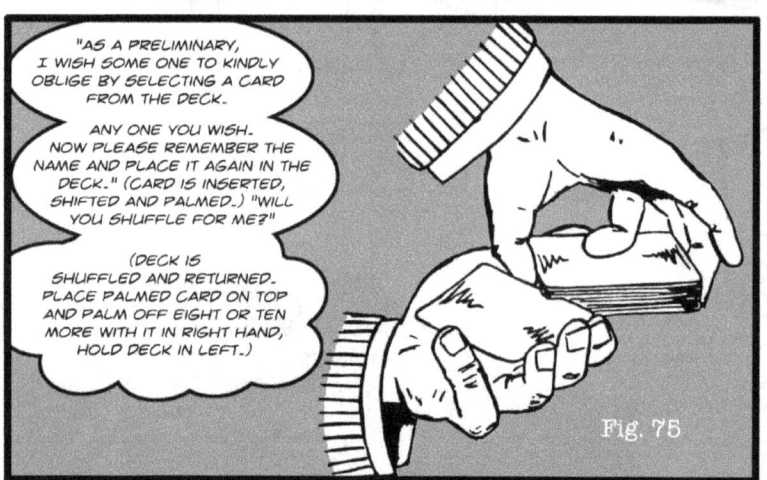

"AS A PRELIMINARY, I WISH SOME ONE TO KINDLY OBLIGE BY SELECTING A CARD FROM THE DECK.

ANY ONE YOU WISH. NOW PLEASE REMEMBER THE NAME AND PLACE IT AGAIN IN THE DECK." (CARD IS INSERTED, SHIFTED AND PALMED.) "WILL YOU SHUFFLE FOR ME?"

(DECK IS SHUFFLED AND RETURNED. PLACE PALMED CARD ON TOP AND PALM OFF EIGHT OR TEN MORE WITH IT IN RIGHT HAND, HOLD DECK IN LEFT.)

Fig. 75

"NOW TO ILLUSTRATE THE POINT IN QUESTION, LADIES AND GENTLEMEN, I AM GOING TO CAUSE THESE CARDS TO FLY UP MY SLEEVE AND OUT THROUGH THE ARMHOLE HERE."

(INDICATE PLACE BY THRUSTING THE RIGHT HAND INTO THE SHOULDER OF COAT, AND LEAVE PALMED CARDS THERE.)

"NOW, ATTENTION, PLEASE, AND YOU MAY SEE THEM FLY, OR IF YOU DO NOT SEE THEM, YOU MAY HEAR THEM."

FIRST CARD, GO!"

(CLICK CORNER OF DECK WITH LEFT LITTLE FINGER, CARELESSLY SHOW RIGHT HAND EMPTY, PASSING IT RATHER QUICKLY UNDER COAT TO SHOULDER AND PRODUCE BOTTOM CARD. SHOW IT AND THROW ON TABLE.)

"WELL, YOU SEE THE FIRST CARD OBEYED ME. SECOND CARD, PASS!" (PRODUCE ANOTHER FROM BOTTOM.)

"THIRD CARD!" (PRODUCE; EACH TIME CLICKING DECK WITH FINGER AS CARDS ARE ORDERED TO PASS, AND SHOWING CARDS AS PRODUCED.)

"BUT WE HAVE HAD A CARD SELECTED AND SHUFFLED IN THE DECK, AND THOUGH WE HAVE NO IDEA WHERE IT IS I SHALL COMMAND IT TO FLY UP MY SLEEVE AT WHATEVER NUMBER YOU MAY ELECT.

WHAT SHALL IT BE—FOUR, FIVE, SIX OR SEVEN? THE SIXTH? VERY WELL. AS THREE CARDS HAVE ALREADY PASSED, THE SELECTED CARD SHALL BE THE THIRD ONE.

PASS!" (PRODUCE.) "PASS!" (PRODUCE.)

"OH, WHAT IS THE NAME OF THE CARD YOU SELECTED? JACK OF HEARTS! WELL, JACK OF HEARTS, IT IS YOUR TURN, SIR.

YOU WILL PLEASE OBLIGE THE COMPANY BY FLYING UP MY SLEEVE."

(PRODUCE TOP CARD, SHOWING IT TO BE THE ONE CALLED UPON.)

As the performer makes the first transfer, he simply adds one to the number moved, one being the position of the card that otherwise would be turned, and he has the position for the turn when the company makes the first transfer.

Much effect may be obtained with this trick if the proper address and by-play are indulged.

The performer may affect to accomplish the feat by mind reading, and increase the interest by failing to fathom the subtlety of some lady's intellectual faculty, and easily wresting the secret from the coarser calibre of some gentleman, even against his will; and by pretending to have determined the number transferred before turning the card, and making the finding of the particular card also dependent upon some extraordinary power.

The trick is one of the very best of those NOT requiring sleight of hand.

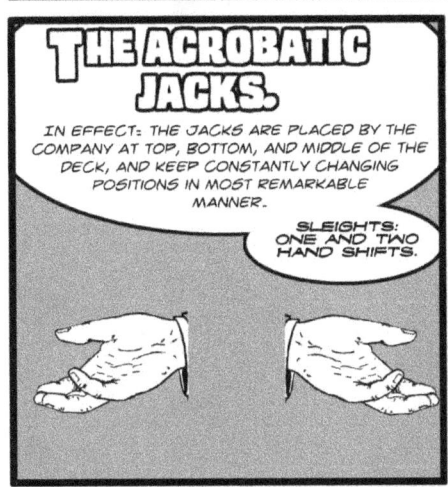

THE ACROBATIC JACKS.

IN EFFECT: The jacks are placed by the company at top, bottom, and middle of the deck, and keep constantly changing positions in most remarkable manner.

SLEIGHTS: ONE AND TWO HAND SHIFTS.

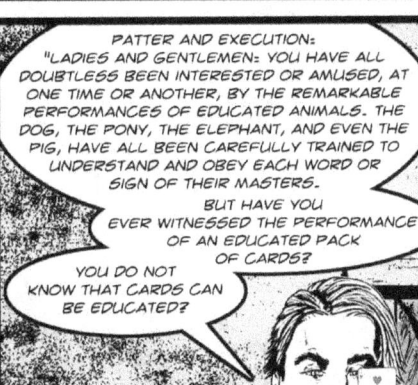

PATTER AND EXECUTION:
"Ladies and gentlemen: You have all doubtless been interested or amused, at one time or another, by the remarkable performances of educated animals. The dog, the pony, the elephant, and even the pig, have all been carefully trained to understand and obey each word or sign of their masters.

But have you ever witnessed the performance of an educated pack of cards?

You do not know that cards can be educated?

I assure you that it is quite possible, and I shall demonstrate the truth of my assertion.

Moreover, I have discovered in my efforts to educate my fifty-two pupils, that they, like the members of any other family, possess certain individual characteristics or temperaments, and I have endeavored to develop the special talents of each, in the direction most in keeping with the natural bent.

"I shall select the four jacks for the purpose of illustrating how an original athletic tendency that was early manifested by them has been developed by a system of training, until they have acquired a degree of skill in acrobatic feats that is truly remarkable. I wish two ladies or gentlemen in the audience to assist me, by each holding two of the jacks."

(Give two red jacks to spectator, whom we shall designate as A., and two black jacks to second spectator, whom we shall call B. Then to A.)

"Will you, sir, place one of the red jacks on top of the deck? Thank you. And will you (to B.) place one of the black jacks in the middle of the deck?"

(Open pack with left thumb bookwise, ready for the "Charlier shift," and when jack is inserted shift packets.)

"Now, ladies and gentlemen, we have a red jack on top, and a black jack in the middle, and as a first display of their intelligence and training, I shall order them to change places. Ready. GO!"

Fig. 65

(Click deck with little finger and show change has taken place. Hand jacks back to A. and B.)

"You see that they are quite active and very obedient. We shall try them again and place them farther apart. (To A.) Place your red jack at the bottom. (To B.) Place your black jack on top. Now observe, I shall not touch the cards,"

(Make gesture with the right hand as if to show that this hand would be the one necessarily employed, and as attention is attracted to it, shift with the left.)

"But shall command the jacks to perform a somersault from the top and bottom and meet in the middle. Attention. GO!"

Fig. 53

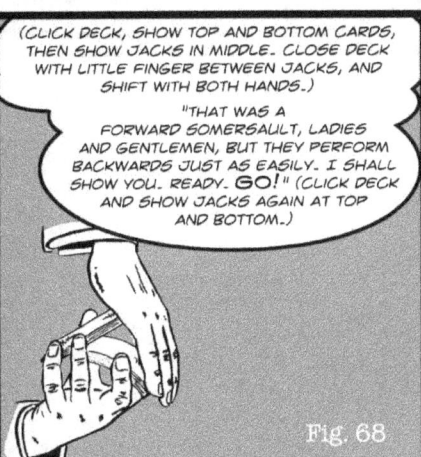

(Click deck, show top and bottom cards, then show jacks in middle. Close deck with little finger between jacks, and shift with both hands.)

"That was a forward somersault, ladies and gentlemen, but they perform backwards just as easily. I shall show you. Ready. GO!" (Click deck and show jacks again at top and bottom.)

Fig. 68

"I TRUST I HAVE IMPRESSED YOU SOMEWHAT WITH THE INTELLIGENCE AND AGILITY THE JACKS POSSESS IN THEMSELVES, BUT FOR FEAR YOU MAY FANCY THAT I HAVE ANYTHING TO DO WITH THEIR PERFORMANCE, I SHALL CALL UPON ALL FOUR JACKS TO EXECUTE THEIR GROUND AND LOFTY TUMBLING AT THE SAME TIME, AND I NEED NOT SAY TO YOU, LADIES AND GENTLEMEN, THAT HOWEVER CLEVER I MIGHT BE, I COULD NOT POSSIBLY, OF MY OWN POWER, INSTANTANEOUSLY CHANGE THE POSITIONS OF FOUR CARDS AT FOUR DIFFERENT POINTS."

(GIVE BACK JACKS TO A. AND B., AND HAVE A. PLACE HIS AT TOP AND BOTTOM, AND B. PLACE HIS TWO IN MIDDLE. INSERT LITTLE FINGER BETWEEN MIDDLE JACKS AND MAKE SHIFT WITH BOTH HANDS.)

"NOW, PLEASE REMEMBER THE ORDER.

Fig. 49

THE TWO RED JACKS ARE AT THE TOP AND BOTTOM, AND THE TWO BLACK JACKS ARE IN THE MIDDLE. THIS TIME I SHALL ORDER THE FOUR TO PLAY LEAP-FROG, AND EACH TAKE THE PLACE OF THE OTHER. READY. GO!"

(MAKE CLICK AND SHOW THE CHANGES HAVE TAKEN PLACE.)

"I CANNOT DOUBT, AFTER THIS DEMONSTRATION, THAT YOU ARE QUITE SATISFIED THE JACKS HAVE BEEN FAIRLY WELL TRAINED; AND I AM NOW GOING TO MAKE THEM PERFORM THEIR ACROBATIC FEAT VERY SLOWLY, SO THAT YOU MAY ALL SEE JUST HOW IT IS DONE." (GIVE BACK JACKS TO A. AND B. THEN TO A.)

"PLACE YOUR TWO RED JACKS AGAIN AT THE TOP AND BOTTOM;" (THEN TO B.)

"AND NOW WE SHALL HAVE YOURS AGAIN IN THE MIDDLE. BUT STOP! ON SECOND THOUGHT, AS YOU ARE TO SEE HOW IT IS DONE, I SHALL HAVE THE JACKS EXECUTE THEIR SOMERSAULTS WHILE THE DECK IS IN YOUR HANDS.

I ASSURE YOU THEY WILL PERFORM EQUALLY WELL, AND THE MOMENT YOU PLACE YOUR CARDS IN THE MIDDLE I WISH YOU TO HOLD THE DECK YOURSELF"

(APPARENTLY CUT DECK IN THE MIDDLE, BUT REALLY MAKE TWO-HANDED SHIFT WITHOUT BRINGING THE TWO PACKETS TOGETHER AGAIN, HOLDING THE RIGHT-HAND PACKET A FEW INCHES OVER THE LEFT WHEN SHIFT IS MADE. HAVE JACKS PLACED BETWEEN, AND IMMEDIATELY CLOSE PACKETS, PUTTING DECK IN B.'S HANDS.)

"NOW, SIR, DON'T HOLD THEM TOO FIRMLY, AND WATCH THEM PERFORM. I SHALL ORDER ALL FOUR TO COME TOGETHER AT THE MIDDLE. ALL READY. GO! DID YOU SEE THEM GO? NOR EVEN FEEL THEM GO? THAT IS STRANGE, FOR THEY CERTAINLY OBEYED ME. LOOK AT THE TOP AND BOTTOM CARDS. THEY HAVE GONE! NOW LOOK IN THE MIDDLE AND YOU WILL FIND THEM ALL TOGETHER AS COMMANDED."

A MIND-READING TRICK.

SLEIGHTS: STOCK SHUFFLE. EXECUTION AND PATTER: "LADIES AND GENTLEMEN, I SHALL NEXT ATTEMPT AN EXPERIMENT IN MIND-READING, AND THOUGH I DO NOT CLAIM TO BE AN ADEPT IN THE ART, I HAVE MANAGED TO OBTAIN AN UNDERSTANDING OF ITS FUNDAMENTAL PRINCIPLES, AND I SHALL ENDEAVOR TO DEMONSTRATE THAT UNDER FAVORABLE CONDITIONS I CAN ACTUALLY READ THE THOUGHT THAT IS MOST PROMINENT IN THE MIND OF A WILLING SUBJECT.

I WISH SOME GENTLEMAN IN THE AUDIENCE WHO IS DESIROUS OF GIVING MY ABILITY A FAIR AND IMPARTIAL TEST, TO TAKE THIS DECK OF CARDS IN HIS OWN HANDS AND SELECT ANY FOUR HE MAY WISH FOR THE PURPOSE OF MY EXPERIMENT." (GIVE DECK TO SPECTATOR, WHO SELECTS FOUR CARDS AT WILL, AND TAKE BACK DECK.)

"NOW, SIR, WILL YOU PLEASE MAKE A MENTAL NOTE OF ANY ONE CARD OF THE FOUR YOU HAVE SELECTED, AND AS AN AID TO IMPRESS IT MOST FIRMLY, THINK OF THE ONE THAT TO YOU MAY APPEAR THE MOST EASILY REMEMBERED.

IF YOU CAN ASSOCIATE ONE OF THEM WITH A PROMINENT DATE, OR SOME INCIDENT IN YOUR OWN LIFE, SO MUCH THE BETTER; AND, IF POSSIBLE, DISABUSE YOUR MIND COMPLETELY OF THE OTHER THREE. HAVE YOU DONE THIS? THANK YOU.

NOW INSERT THE FOUR ANYWHERE IN THE DECK."

(HAVE CARDS REPLACED IN MIDDLE, FORM BREAK ABOVE, WITH RIGHT THUMB AT INNER END, TURN ON SIDE IN LEFT HAND IN POSITION FOR BLIND SHUFFLE. UNDER-CUT TO ABOUT HALF PORTION ABOVE BREAK, SHUFFLE OFF TO BREAK, RUN TWO, IN-JOG RUNNING, SAY, SEVENTEEN, OUT-JOG AND SHUFFLE OFF. UNDER CUT TO IN-JOG AND THROW ON TOP.

UNDER-CUT TO OUT-JOG, RUN SEVEN AND THROW BALANCE ON TOP. THIS ACTION PLACES TWO OF THE SELECTED CARDS THE NINTH AND TENTH FROM THE TOP, AND THE OTHER TWO THE EIGHTEENTH AND NINETEENTH.)

"NOW, LADIES AND GENTLEMEN, I HAVE DOUBTLESS QUITE SATISFIED YOU, AND MOST CERTAINLY MYSELF, THAT THE FOUR CARDS DRAWN, INCLUDING THE PARTICULAR ONE THOUGHT OF, ARE HOPELESSLY LOST IN THE SHUFFLE; BUT BEFORE ATTEMPTING TO READ THE MIND OF THE GENTLEMAN WHO IS SO KINDLY ASSISTING ME IN THE EXPERIMENT, I WISH TO BE ASSURED THAT HE HAS GOT THE CARD FIRMLY ESTABLISHED IN HIS MEMORY.

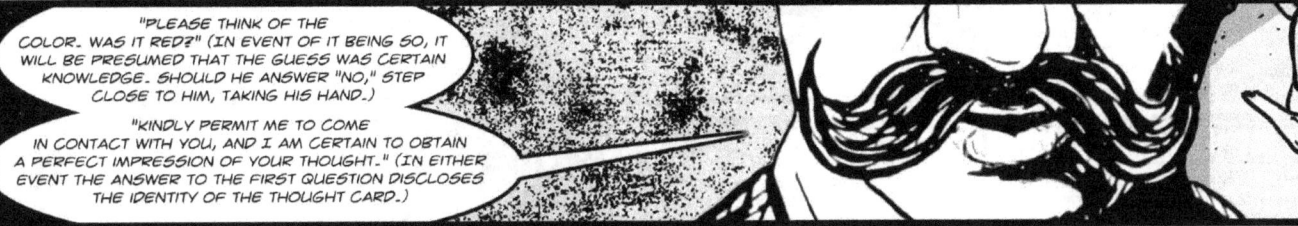

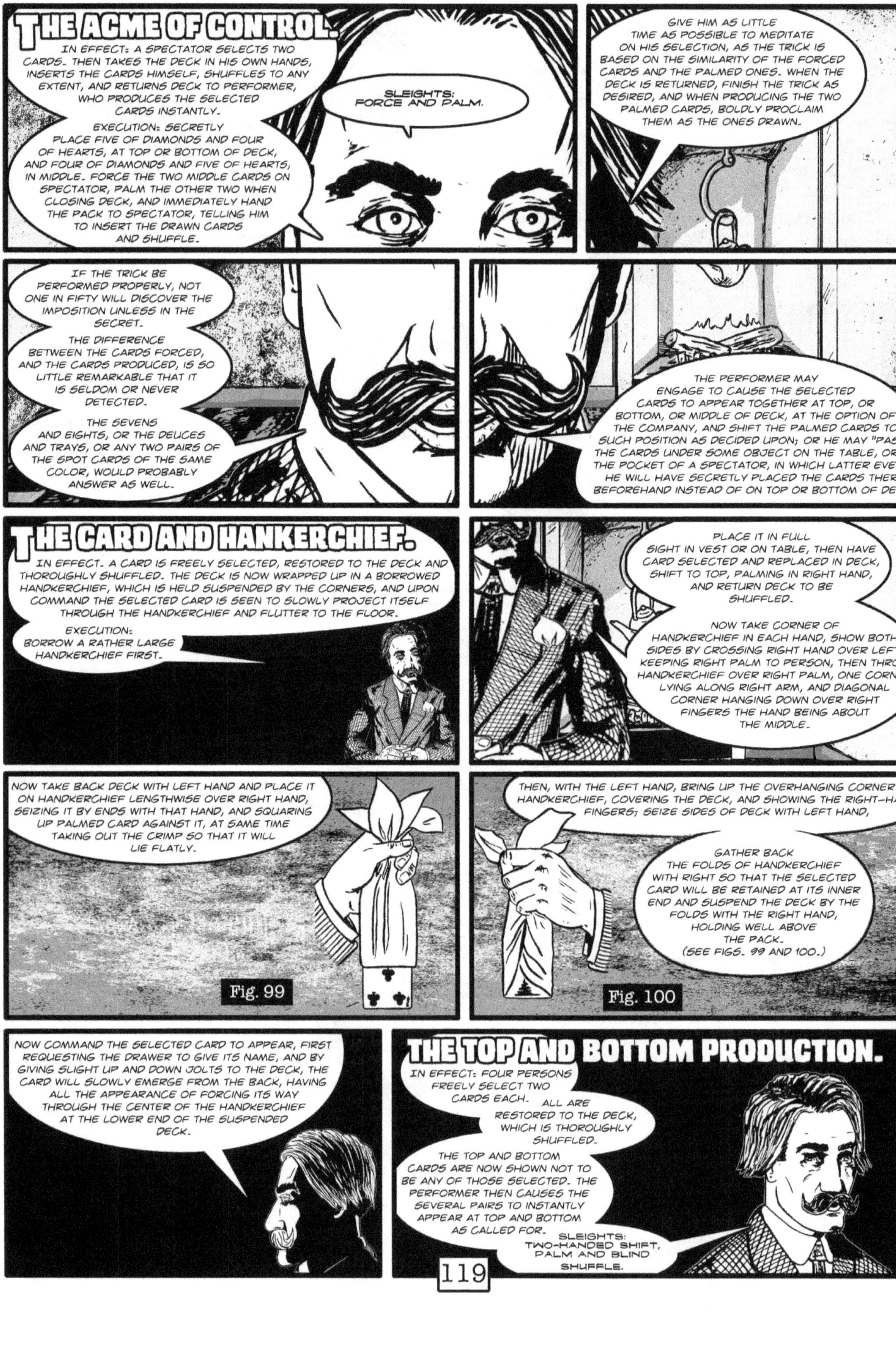

THE ACME OF CONTROL.

IN EFFECT: A SPECTATOR SELECTS TWO CARDS. THEN TAKES THE DECK IN HIS OWN HANDS, INSERTS THE CARDS HIMSELF, SHUFFLES TO ANY EXTENT, AND RETURNS DECK TO PERFORMER, WHO PRODUCES THE SELECTED CARDS INSTANTLY.

EXECUTION: SECRETLY PLACE FIVE OF DIAMONDS AND FOUR OF HEARTS, AT TOP OR BOTTOM OF DECK, AND FOUR OF DIAMONDS AND FIVE OF HEARTS, IN MIDDLE. FORCE THE TWO MIDDLE CARDS ON SPECTATOR, PALM THE OTHER TWO WHEN CLOSING DECK, AND IMMEDIATELY HAND THE PACK TO SPECTATOR, TELLING HIM TO INSERT THE DRAWN CARDS AND SHUFFLE.

SLEIGHTS: FORCE AND PALM.

GIVE HIM AS LITTLE TIME AS POSSIBLE TO MEDITATE ON HIS SELECTION, AS THE TRICK IS BASED ON THE SIMILARITY OF THE FORCED CARDS AND THE PALMED ONES. WHEN THE DECK IS RETURNED, FINISH THE TRICK AS DESIRED, AND WHEN PRODUCING THE TWO PALMED CARDS, BOLDLY PROCLAIM THEM AS THE ONES DRAWN.

IF THE TRICK BE PERFORMED PROPERLY, NOT ONE IN FIFTY WILL DISCOVER THE IMPOSITION UNLESS IN THE SECRET.

THE DIFFERENCE BETWEEN THE CARDS FORCED, AND THE CARDS PRODUCED, IS SO LITTLE REMARKABLE THAT IT IS SELDOM OR NEVER DETECTED.

THE SEVENS AND EIGHTS, OR THE DEUCES AND TRAYS, OR ANY TWO PAIRS OF THE SPOT CARDS OF THE SAME COLOR, WOULD PROBABLY ANSWER AS WELL.

THE PERFORMER MAY ENGAGE TO CAUSE THE SELECTED CARDS TO APPEAR TOGETHER AT TOP, OR BOTTOM, OR MIDDLE OF DECK, AT THE OPTION OF THE COMPANY, AND SHIFT THE PALMED CARDS TO SUCH POSITION AS DECIDED UPON; OR HE MAY "PASS" THE CARDS UNDER SOME OBJECT ON THE TABLE, OR TO THE POCKET OF A SPECTATOR, IN WHICH LATTER EVENTS HE WILL HAVE SECRETLY PLACED THE CARDS THERE BEFOREHAND INSTEAD OF ON TOP OR BOTTOM OF DECK.

THE CARD AND HANKERCHIEF.

IN EFFECT. A CARD IS FREELY SELECTED, RESTORED TO THE DECK AND THOROUGHLY SHUFFLED. THE DECK IS NOW WRAPPED UP IN A BORROWED HANDKERCHIEF, WHICH IS HELD SUSPENDED BY THE CORNERS, AND UPON COMMAND THE SELECTED CARD IS SEEN TO SLOWLY PROJECT ITSELF THROUGH THE HANDKERCHIEF AND FLUTTER TO THE FLOOR.

EXECUTION: BORROW A RATHER LARGE HANDKERCHIEF FIRST.

PLACE IT IN FULL SIGHT IN VEST OR ON TABLE, THEN HAVE CARD SELECTED AND REPLACED IN DECK, SHIFT TO TOP, PALMING IN RIGHT HAND, AND RETURN DECK TO BE SHUFFLED.

NOW TAKE CORNER OF HANDKERCHIEF IN EACH HAND, SHOW BOTH SIDES BY CROSSING RIGHT HAND OVER LEFT, KEEPING RIGHT PALM TO PERSON, THEN THROW HANDKERCHIEF OVER RIGHT PALM, ONE CORNER LYING ALONG RIGHT ARM, AND DIAGONAL CORNER HANGING DOWN OVER RIGHT FINGERS THE HAND BEING ABOUT THE MIDDLE.

NOW TAKE BACK DECK WITH LEFT HAND AND PLACE IT ON HANDKERCHIEF LENGTHWISE OVER RIGHT HAND, SEIZING IT BY ENDS WITH THAT HAND, AND SQUARING UP PALMED CARD AGAINST IT, AT SAME TIME TAKING OUT THE CRIMP SO THAT IT WILL LIE FLATLY.

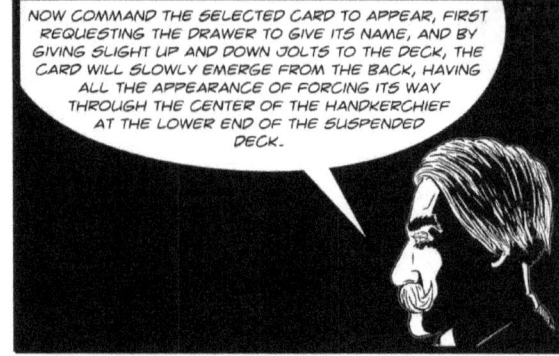

Fig. 99

THEN, WITH THE LEFT HAND, BRING UP THE OVERHANGING CORNER OF HANDKERCHIEF, COVERING THE DECK, AND SHOWING THE RIGHT-HAND FINGERS; SEIZE SIDES OF DECK WITH LEFT HAND,

GATHER BACK THE FOLDS OF HANDKERCHIEF WITH RIGHT SO THAT THE SELECTED CARD WILL BE RETAINED AT ITS INNER END AND SUSPEND THE DECK BY THE FOLDS WITH THE RIGHT HAND, HOLDING WELL ABOVE THE PACK. (SEE FIGS. 99 AND 100.)

Fig. 100

NOW COMMAND THE SELECTED CARD TO APPEAR, FIRST REQUESTING THE DRAWER TO GIVE ITS NAME, AND BY GIVING SLIGHT UP AND DOWN JOLTS TO THE DECK, THE CARD WILL SLOWLY EMERGE FROM THE BACK, HAVING ALL THE APPEARANCE OF FORCING ITS WAY THROUGH THE CENTER OF THE HANDKERCHIEF AT THE LOWER END OF THE SUSPENDED DECK.

THE TOP AND BOTTOM PRODUCTION.

IN EFFECT: FOUR PERSONS FREELY SELECT TWO CARDS EACH. ALL ARE RESTORED TO THE DECK, WHICH IS THOROUGHLY SHUFFLED.

THE TOP AND BOTTOM CARDS ARE NOW SHOWN NOT TO BE ANY OF THOSE SELECTED. THE PERFORMER THEN CAUSES THE SEVERAL PAIRS TO INSTANTLY APPEAR AT TOP AND BOTTOM AS CALLED FOR.

SLEIGHTS: TWO-HANDED SHIFT, PALM AND BLIND SHUFFLE.

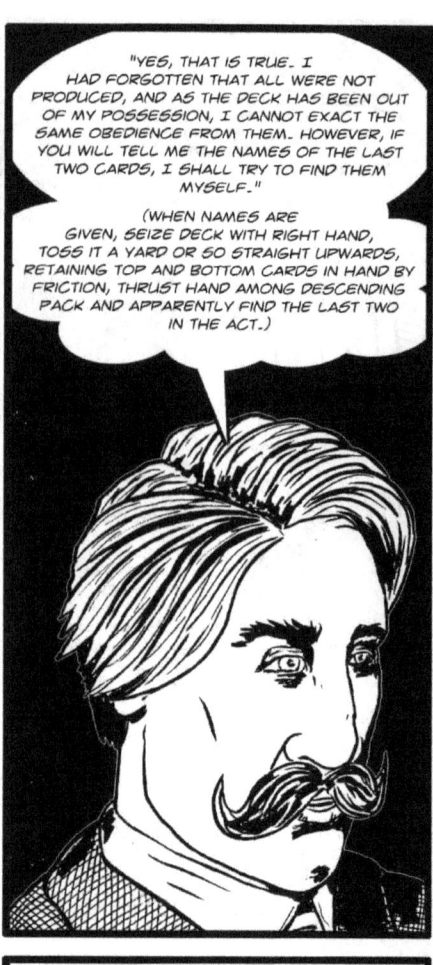

"YES, THAT IS TRUE. I HAD FORGOTTEN THAT ALL WERE NOT PRODUCED, AND AS THE DECK HAS BEEN OUT OF MY POSSESSION, I CANNOT EXACT THE SAME OBEDIENCE FROM THEM. HOWEVER, IF YOU WILL TELL ME THE NAMES OF THE LAST TWO CARDS, I SHALL TRY TO FIND THEM MYSELF."

(WHEN NAMES ARE GIVEN, SEIZE DECK WITH RIGHT HAND, TOSS IT A YARD OR SO STRAIGHT UPWARDS, RETAINING TOP AND BOTTOM CARDS IN HAND BY FRICTION, THRUST HAND AMONG DESCENDING PACK AND APPARENTLY FIND THE LAST TWO IN THE ACT.)

THE THREE ACES.

IN EFFECT: THE ACE OF DIAMONDS, ACE OF CLUBS AND ACE OF SPADES ARE SHOWN TO THE COMPANY AND LAID FACE DOWN ON THE TABLE.

THEN ONE IS PICKED UP AND INSERTED IN THE MIDDLE OF THE DECK, ANOTHER IS PLACED ON THE BOTTOM, AND THE THIRD IS PLACED ON THE TOP.

A SINGLE TRUE CUT IS NOW MADE AND THE THREE ACES ARE FOUND TOGETHER.

SLEIGHT: PREARRANGEMENT.

EXECUTION: SECRETLY PLACE THE ACE OF DIAMONDS ON TOP OF THE DECK.

ARRANGE THE OTHER THREE ACES IN THE LEFT HAND, FANWISE, FACE UP, THE ACE OF HEARTS BELOW THE OTHER TWO, AND SHOWING IN THE MIDDLE.

THE FIGURE OF THE HEART IS INVERTED AND SHOWS AT THE ANGLE MADE BY THE OTHER CARDS, SO THAT THE PART SEEN IS DIAMOND-SHAPED.

THE CORNER OF THE ACE ON THE LEFT OF THE FAN JUST COVERS THE SMALL HEART FIGURE OF THE INDEX, BUT FULLY EXPOSES THE SMALL LETTER "A." (SEE FIG. 101.)

THIS ARRANGEMENT CAN BE MADE IN A MOMENT.

THE APPEARANCE IS MOST INNOCENT AND SURPRISINGLY DECEPTIVE.

Fig. 101

TURN THE FACES TO THE COMPANY, AND THEN LAY THE THREE CARDS FACE DOWN ON THE TABLE, STILL IN THE SAME FAN POSITION, AND WITH THE SAME HAND. NOW TAKE UP THE DECK, AND, IF DESIRED, EXECUTE A BLIND SHUFFLE, RETAINING TOP ACE.

Fig. 3

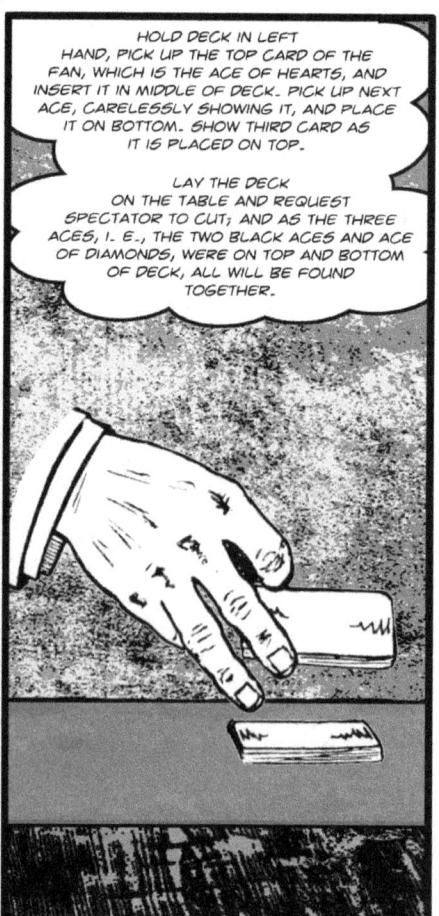

HOLD DECK IN LEFT HAND, PICK UP THE TOP CARD OF THE FAN, WHICH IS THE ACE OF HEARTS, AND INSERT IT IN MIDDLE OF DECK. PICK UP NEXT ACE, CARELESSLY SHOWING IT, AND PLACE IT ON BOTTOM. SHOW THIRD CARD AS IT IS PLACED ON TOP.

LAY THE DECK ON THE TABLE AND REQUEST SPECTATOR TO CUT; AND AS THE THREE ACES, I. E., THE TWO BLACK ACES AND ACE OF DIAMONDS, WERE ON TOP AND BOTTOM OF DECK, ALL WILL BE FOUND TOGETHER.

The Card and Hat.

IN EFFECT: A borrowed hat is placed upon the table.

A card is now freely selected and given to a second spectator to hold. Attention is now drawn to the hat, which is shown to be empty, and it is again placed on the table, but crown up.

The selected card is then restored to the deck by the spectator, who is permitted to take the deck in his own hands.

The performer now exercises very remarkable powers by first determining the name of the selected card, and then causing it to wing an invisible flight from the deck to a position beneath the hat on the table, where it is found by a spectator.

SLEIGHTS: Top change and palm.

EXECUTION: Borrow the hat first and place it rim up on the table.

Have a card selected by spectator on the left. Take it from him with the right hand, and when turning to spectator on the right, make "top change," and request second spectator to hold the card between his two palms; which will prevent him from looking at it.

Fig. 80

Now palm top card in right hand and give deck to first spectator to hold.

Fig. 38

Step towards table, getting glimpse of palmed card, and pick up the hat with right hand, fingers well inside, thumb across rim, calling attention to the fact that it is empty, and showing the inside.

Now turn the rim down and place the hat again upon the table, working the palmed card up along the inside with the fingers, and releasing it as the hat is laid down.

Care must be taken to leave no crimp in the card.

Now take deck from first spectator, request second spectator to hold it in the hand that happens to be uppermost.

Then take the card from his other hand and insert it in the deck, and have spectator shuffle thoroughly.

As the action is now complete, make by-play of determining the name of the drawn card, by tracing the very faint impression that it left on the palm of spectator who held it; and cause it to speed from the deck, under the hat, visibly if desired, expressing surprise that no one sees it going, and have spectator raise the hat to prove there is no hocus-pocus.

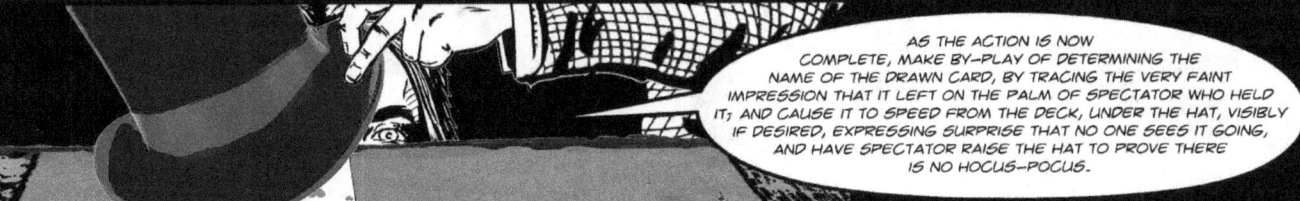

HOW I STAYED TRUE TO THE ORIGINAL.
(THE PROCESS)

THE GOAL WAS TO KEEP THE ORIGINAL WORK INTACT, WHILE ALSO FULLY RESTRUCTURING AND PRESENTING IN AN ENTIRELY NEW MANNER. SIMPLE, RIGHT? BELOW IS A PROCESS DESCRIPTION THAT SOMEHOW MAKES IT ALL SEEM A WHOLE LOT EASIER AND SO MUCH LESS TIME CONSUMING THAN IT ACTUALLY WAS.

ORIGINAL SCAN OF FIGURE 53 (PART OF THE ERDNASE ONE-HANDED SHIFT,) POST CLEAN-UP AND ENLARGEMENT. THEN THESE CLEANED, ORIGINAL FIGURES WERE CHANGED FROM BLACK TO LIGHT BLUE AND PRINTED.

Fig. 53

INKING CAME NEXT. USING BLACK INK, THE BLUE FIGURES WERE TOUCHED UP, DETAIL AND DEPTH WERE ADDED. SINCE THE ORIGINAL FIGURES ARE BLUE, AND THE TOUCH-UP FIGURES ARE BLACK, ALL THE OLDER LINE-WORK DISAPPEARS WHEN SCANNED BACK IN AFTER INKING, LEAVING THE NEW BLACK LINES ONLY.

Fig. 53

HERE IS THE SCANNED AND CLEANED UP FINAL IMAGE OF FIGURE 53. NOW IT IS READY TO BE SCALED BACK DOWN FOR INSERTION ONTO AN ARM. THIS SOMEWHAT LENGTHY AND REPETITIVE PROCESS ALLOWED FOR US TO KEEP THE EXACT DRAWINGS FROM THE ORIGINAL, BUT IN A STYLE THAT MATCHES THE REST OF THE BOOK.

THE FINAL PANEL: AFTER COMBINING THE NEEDED ERDNASE BODY PARTS, I ADD A BACKGROUND AND LETTERING. (LAST COMES BALLOONS.)

Fig. 53

THE FIG.S

THE MOST DAUNTING PART OF THIS ENTIRE PROJECT WAS RE-INKING THE ORIGINAL FIGURE DRAWINGS. IT WAS PROBABLY THE MOST FUN AS WELL. BELOW IS WHAT A PAGE OF THE NEW LOOKS LIKE AND NEXT IS A PAGE OF THE ORIGINALS.

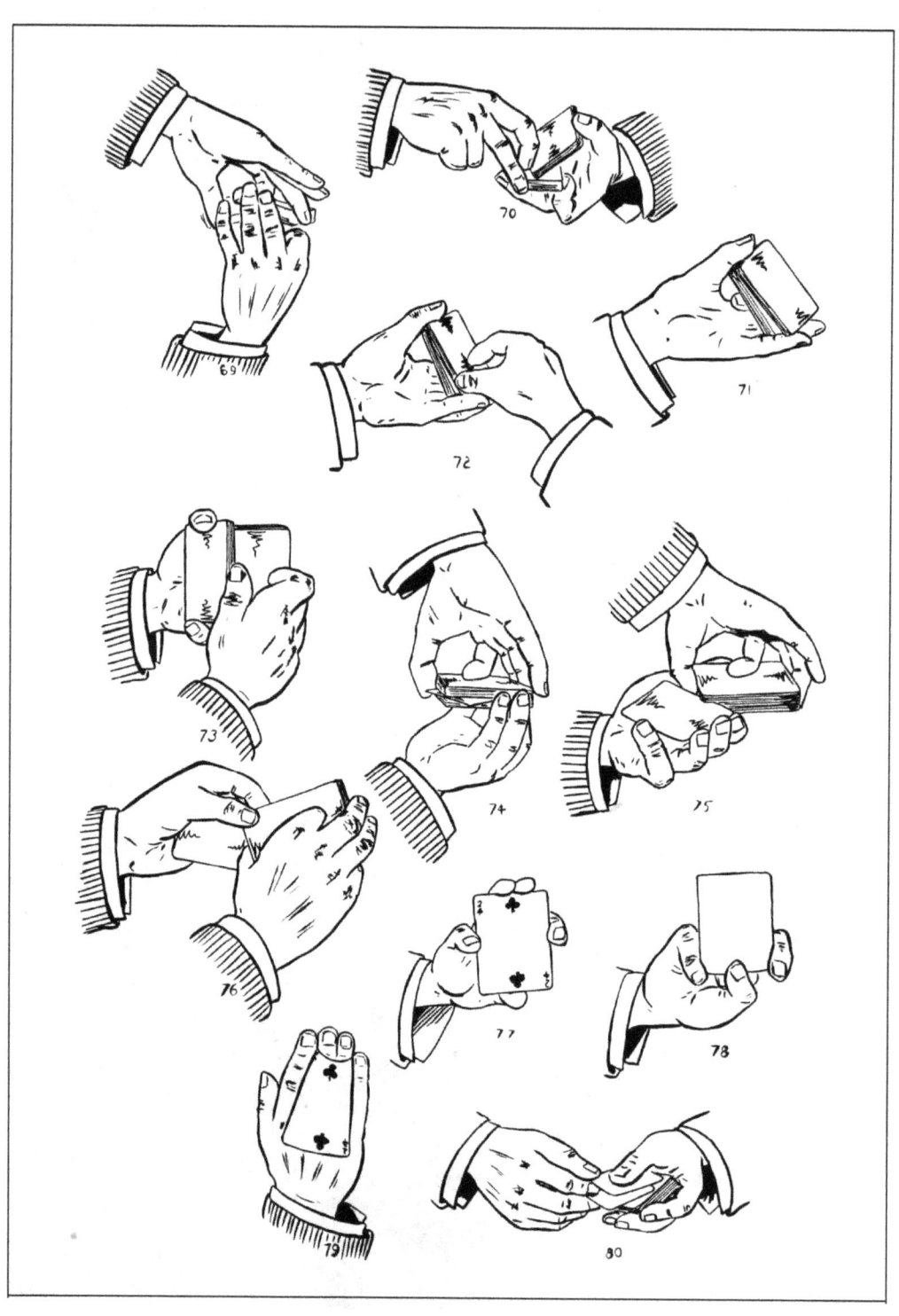

THE FIG.S

THESE ARE "THE ORIGINALS". I HAD TO MANIPULATE THEM A LITTLE WHICH ADDED SOME ROUGH EDGES TO THE LINE WORK. BUT THEN ALL OF THIS WAS TURNED LIGHT BLUE, SO IT REALLY DIDN'T MATTER. NEW PENCIL WORK WAS DONE, AND THEN THE INK TO MAKE WHAT YOU SAW ON THE PREVIOUS PAGE.

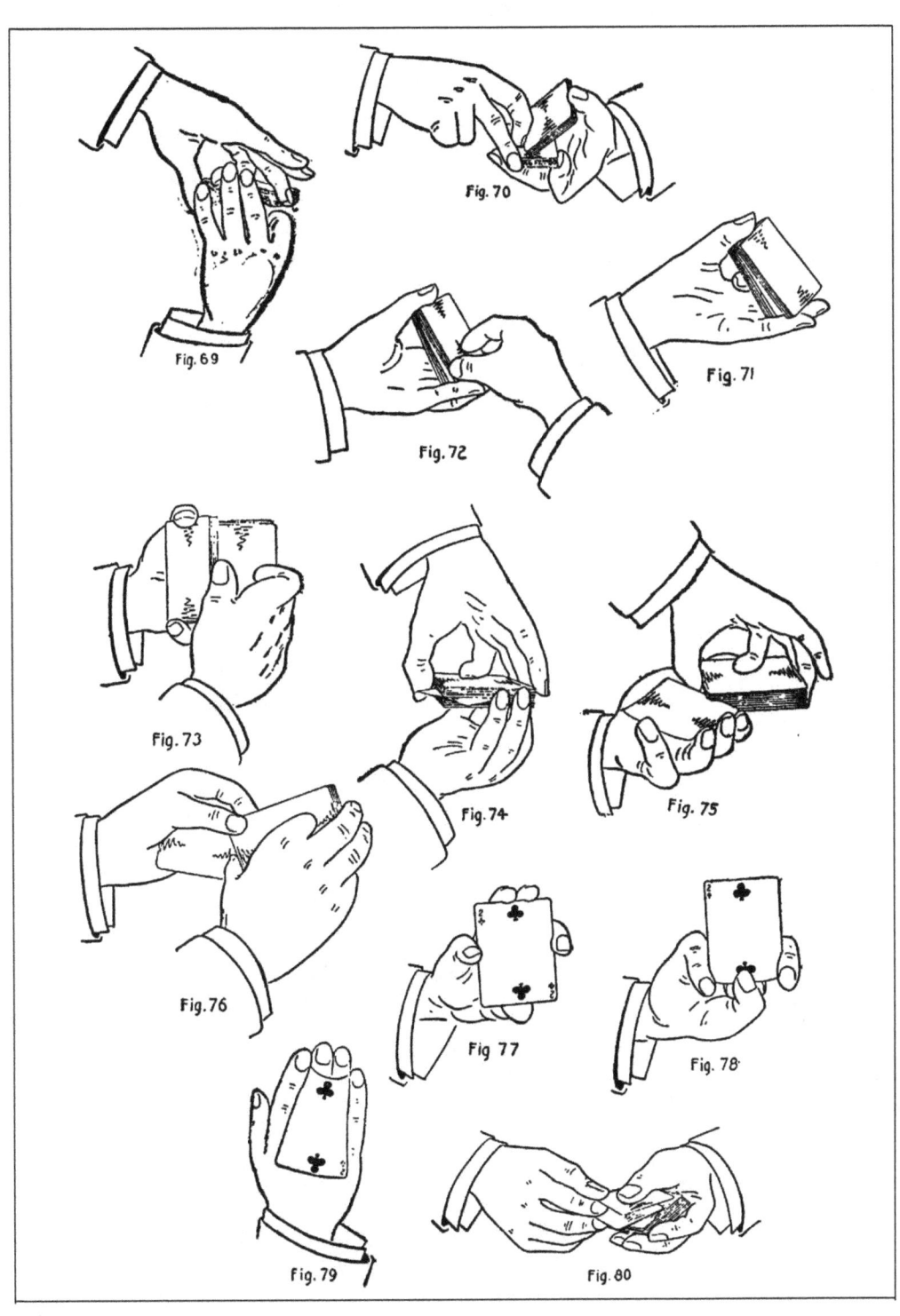

POINT B HANDS

THE EXPERT REQUIRED A LOT OF HAND DRAWINGS. I CALLED THESE "POINT B" HANDS. BELOW IS JUST A SNAP-SHOT OF THE VARIOUS HANDS THAT HAD TO BE CREATED TO COMPLETE THIS PROJECT.

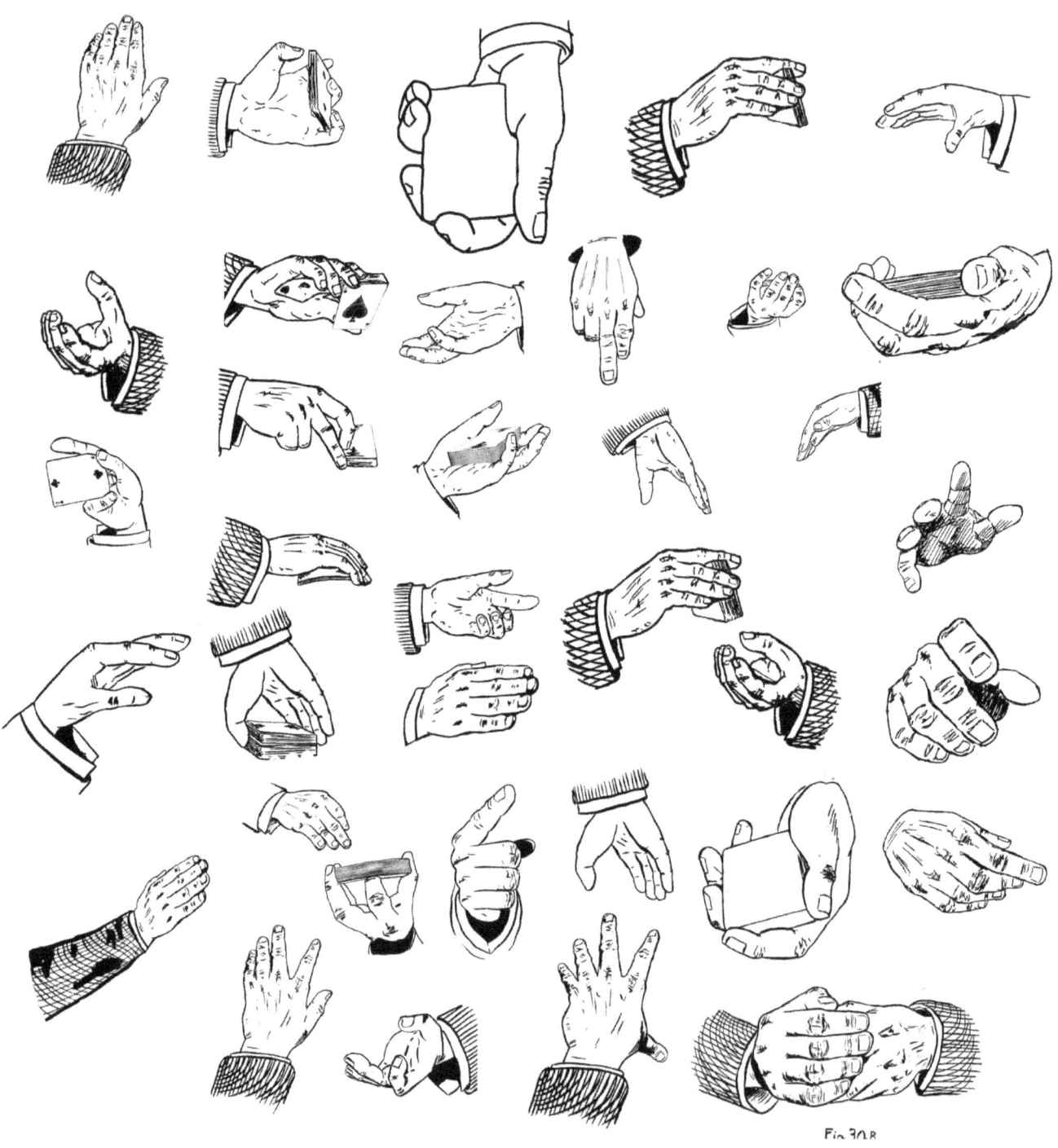

DR. STRERDNASE

ONE NIGHT I DREW ERDNASE AS DR. STRANGE. THAT SIMPLE. MIGHT EVEN FINISH IT ONE DAY!

A PORTRAIT
A WARM-UP PIECE I DID ONE DAY OF OUR BELOVED ERDNASE.

MNEMONIC ART

OF COURSE THERE'S MNEMONICS IN HERE! THE BULK OF THE BOOK IS MEANT TO BE SITTING DIRECTLY ACROSS FROM ERDNASE. BUT SOME THINGS NEED TO BE REMEMBERED. THIS STACK IMAGE WAS ESPECIALLY FUN TO FIGURE OUT.

HEADS

WHILE ERDNASE IS ALMOST ENTIRELY SEEN FROM THE WAIST UP, IT REQUIRED A LOT OF WORK TO SIMULATE MOVEMENT. BELOW IS JUST ONE OF A COUPLE DOZEN "SEQUENCES" OF ERDNASE'S FACE WHILE TALKING.

ABOUT THE CREATORS

S.W. ERDNASE - The author as known by a pseudonym. Andrews, Sanders, Galloway are names that have been guessed so far. As time goes on, people suggest that either more evidence could be revealed, while others say it will further disappear to time.

M.D. SMITH - A man named Marshall Smith was given, and accepted, credit as the artist only listed as M.D. Smith. Yet other than an ever changing story, Marshall Smith never actually presented any evidence that he did in fact work on the book. A simple assumption that an artist was hired in the same city the book was published served as the impetus for Martin Gardner's search in Chicago. Most likely, just as S.W. Erdnase was a pseudonym, M.D. Smith is a pseudonym as well. The artist and author could have been a partnership, or even the same person.

DAVID TRUSTMAN - Both writer and artist, the Ringo Award Nominated and Ghastly Award winning comics creator, known for his creations THE RISE and GOD Slap, co-creating the internationally acclaimed MEMORY ARTS Series. For THE EXPERT, David painstakingly reproduced the original figure drawings. A rabid card enthusiast, and perhaps mildly obsessive in personality, he learned the mechanics of each sleight in order to understand the most accurate visual depiction, and then created our Erdnase, and all his many parts.

RESOURCES

Chris Kenner - S.W.E. Shift Download

Orbit Brown's - On the S.W.E. Shift Download.

Darwin Ortiz - Annotated Erdnase

Ricky Smith - Diagonal Palm Shift Download

ConjuringArts.Org

The Expert at the Card Table - Dover Edition

Kevin Reylek